Villa

SHRC

C000136345

Cathy

This book accompanies
the walking stick
Hope you enjoy both in
(your spare time !!!)

love Pat

Village Walks
in
SHROPSHIRE

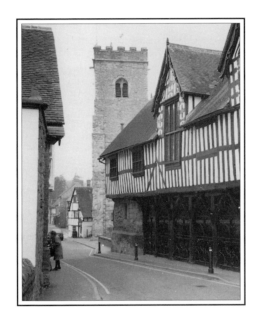

Roy Woodcock

COUNTRYSIDE BOOKS
NEWBURY, BERKSHIRE

COUNTRYSIDE BOOKS
3 Catherine Road
Newbury, Berkshire

ISBN 1 85306 564 1

Designed by Graham Whiteman
Photographs and maps by the author

Front cover photo supplied by Bill Meadows
shows the view from Clunbury Hill

Produced through MRM Associates Ltd., Reading
Typeset by Techniset Typesetters, Newton-le-Willows
Printed by Woolnough Bookbinding Ltd., Irthlingborough

Contents

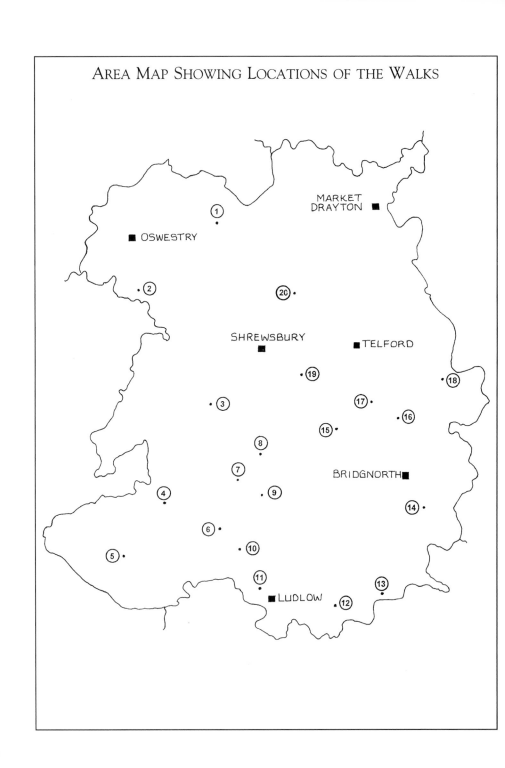

WALK

Publisher's Note

We hope that you obtain considerable enjoyment from this book; great care has been taken in its preparation. Although at the time of publication all routes followed public rights of way or permitted paths, diversion orders can be made and permissions withdrawn.

We cannot of course be held responsible for such diversion orders and any inaccuracies in the text which result from these or any other changes to the routes, nor any damage which might result from walkers trespassing on private property. However, we are anxious that all details covering the walks are kept up to date and would therefore welcome information from readers which would be relevant to future editions.

Introduction

With a population of 420,000 in a total area of 1,347.5 square miles, Shropshire has the smallest population of all the English counties with the exception of Northumberland and Isle of Wight, and a lower population density than all except for Cumbria, North Yorkshire, Northumberland and Lincolnshire. This is a very rural county, with few towns. Shrewsbury is the dominating one and the new town of Telford has become important in recent decades, growing up on the old Shropshire coalfield. Otherwise the towns are small and retain a rural character, as at Ludlow and Market Drayton. It is therefore in its villages that the essential character of Shropshire can be discovered. A large number of villages are not much more than hamlets, often without a church and certainly without a shop or a pub. Others are larger, with a small number of amenities, but there are also a few much bigger villages, which have become market centres for a wide area of countryside. Several of these are large enough to be considered as small towns, yet retain the feeling and characteristics of villages. These include such interesting settlements as Much Wenlock and Craven Arms.

It is also a very undulating county with many short stretches of steep terrain, because of its geological history. In many ways a geologist's dream, with a wide range of variations of rock ages and rock types, its complexity is perhaps a geologist's nightmare as well. The north of the county is mainly low, with New Red sandstones and glacial depositions covering much of the land. The south-east has sandstones (from

the Old Red or Devonian period), but also rocks of the Coal Measure (Carboniferous) series which led to the development of coal mines in the past. The highest point of the county is at Brown Clee Hill (1,780 feet) in the south-east, but it is in the west that most of the hills and high ground are located. It is also in the west that the greatest variety is found with a series of small but steep hills, and many relics of volcanic activity in former times. Volcanic rocks from the pre-Cambrian period (more than 600 million years ago) were eroded to form sediment which when consolidated and uplifted created the rocks of the Long Mynd, amongst the oldest sedimentary rocks anywhere in the world. The oldest rocks of all in the county are the volcanics of the Wrekin and the Stretton Hills.

Because of its geology, Shropshire has been endowed with a variety of minerals and building stones, which have been used in the past as a source of employment as well as great sources of wealth. Signs of industry seem out of place in these quiet rural surroundings, but quarrying, mining and industry have played an important part in the evolution of Shropshire. The Stiperstones, Clee Hill, Wenlock Edge and elsewhere have been the location of quarrying for building stone, with squatter settlements growing up in some of the mining areas. Even more remarkable was the history of mining in the Ironbridge area, the birthplace of the Industrial Revolution.

These 20 circular walks are a wonderful introduction to all that is special about Shropshire. A sketch map accompanies each walk but it is advisable to also carry the appropriate OS map, in either the Landranger or Pathfinder series as noted. Parking places are suggested but do remember to take care and ensure that you park your vehicle in such a way as not to be a nuisance to those who live close by. Separate boxes for each walk indicate where you will find good food and drink on your route and places of interest nearby if you wish to make a day of it!

The county is a walker's paradise with many miles of footpaths including long distance walks such as the Jack Mytton Way (a 60 mile bridleway) and the Shropshire Way which meanders across the county for 165 miles, as well as the Offa's Dyke path now officially designated a National Trail. I hope you will enjoy your walking in this picturesque county, one of Britain's greenest and most scenically attractive, with all those 'blue remembered hills'.

Roy Woodcock

COLEMERE

Length: 3 miles, or 7 miles with an extension to Ellesmere

Getting there: Ellesmere is east of Oswestry and south of Wrexham. Colemere is very tiny and is reached by driving south from Ellesmere along the A528 for just over a mile, and turning left at a crossroads following the sign to Colemere Country Park.

Parking: There is ample parking space at the picnic place in the Country Park.

Map: OS Landranger 126 Shrewsbury and surrounding area or OS Pathfinder 828 Ellesmere East and Prees (GR 436328).

Colemere is only a tiny hamlet, centred round a T junction in the road. The small green, where the signpost points left to the Mere, is overlooked by a few modern houses, but older cottages line the roads both to left and to right. To the right also is a magnificent black and white thatched house and the large Colemere Farm. Turn left at the T junction to reach the two main attractions of the village – the church and the Mere. The Mere is in a nature reserve and has been designated a Site of

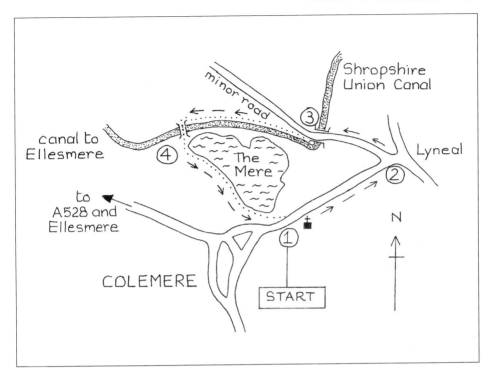

Special Scientific Interest. It is the largest of the nine lakes in this area. The lakes were formed at the end of the Ice Age in hollows left in the mounds of debris dumped by ice. No rivers feed them, and they are dependent on rainfall. The lakes are now an ornithologist's dream, because of their rich diversity of bird life. The Mere is a popular sailing centre and alongside the road overlooking the lake is a car park with picnic area. The Shropshire Union Canal is on the other side of the Mere, once the main transport route in the area but now an important leisure amenity.

Only a gentle stroll, this countryside walk visits the neighbouring village of Lyneal before traversing a totally rural area rich in wild life, especially the water birds on and near the lake. It also follows the towpath of the Shropshire Union Canal for a time, and if you want a longer walk it is simple to continue along the towpath to Ellesmere, before returning around the Mere to Colemere.

FOOD and DRINK

A wide choice of possibilities is available in Ellesmere. If walking to Ellesmere along the canal, continue along Wharf Road and this leads straight to the highly recommended Black Lion (telephone: 01691 622418), a very old pub with excellent food at reasonable prices. The Chef's Special lasagne is very good but there is also a wide choice with salads, jacket potatoes, filled baguettes – something to satisfy all tastes and appetites – and good beer too.

Longboats on the canal at Ellesmere

THE WALK

❶ Walk along the road towards the church, passing the entrance to the old vicarage on the right. St John's church dates from 1870, and serves the village of Lyneal as well as Colemere. The church is built of large sandstone blocks, and is situated on a slight rise from where are good views to the vicarage and the Mere. Continue along the road, with a grassy meadow to the left, and Severn Trent station Lyneal on the right. Beyond here is a very straight road, with an avenue of trees, mainly horse chestnut but some lime. At the end of the straight is Lyneal, and the old school, now a Guide Association Activity Centre where you turn left. But first, before doing so, turn right to walk along the village street, passing a variety of houses including the delightful old Rose Cottage on the right. On the left is Tower Farm with its magnificent chimneys, and less magnificent silage towers.

❷ Walk away from the village, passing the Activity Centre on the right, and head along the country lane to where the road goes over the canal. On the right here is Lyneal Wharf, a canal based holiday centre for people with disabilities.

❸ Turn left at the bridge to walk along

the towpath, which is lined with wild flowers and grasses and together with the woods on the other side of the canal creates a haven for bird and insect life. Follow the towpath, passing a picnic table on the right provided by the Shropshire Union Canal Society, and on beneath bridge number 54. When passing the overflow channel, notice the Mere is much lower than the canal. Pass a couple of buildings on the left, former stables and workshops for the canal, and then reach bridge 55. You could walk on into Ellesmere, along the towpath for a very gentle 2 miles each way and leading into the town at the Canal Wharf.

❹ If not going on into town, turn left along the narrow road, passing the beautiful gardens and lovely thatched house on the

---

PLACES of INTEREST

Ellesmere is the major local attraction, with several interesting old buildings as well as the Wharf, relic of its former days of trading by barge along the Llangollen Canal, a branch of the Shropshire Union. Now the canal is only important for pleasure craft. **Whittington** is 5 miles to the west, and although possibly the home of Dick Whittington is more noted for its castle ruins which dominate the village.

---

right. The road bends left, and then as it bends right, you go left through a kissing gate to follow the woodland path alongside the Mere. This leads through to the boat house beyond which the path divides. To the right are toilets if required, and to the left are the boats and the car park.

LLANYMYNECH

Length: 4 miles

Getting there: Llanymynech is on the A483 south of Oswestry and north of Welshpool, at a crossroads with the B4398.	Parking: In the free car park behind Llanymynech post office.	Maps: OS Landranger 126 Shrewsbury and surrounding area or OS Pathfinder 847 Oswestry South (GR 266209).

The name Llan means 'church' and mynech means 'of the monks'. This ancient village is half in England and half in Wales, standing close to a stone bridge over the River Vyrnwy. There is a strange mixture of buildings, with one black and white house and some use of brick, but also some local limestone which was quarried from the hill overlooking the village from the north. The Montgomery Canal was open from 1796 till 1819, and linked with the Shropshire Union Canal to enable limestone to be transported away from Llanymynech. Before the canal era packhorses

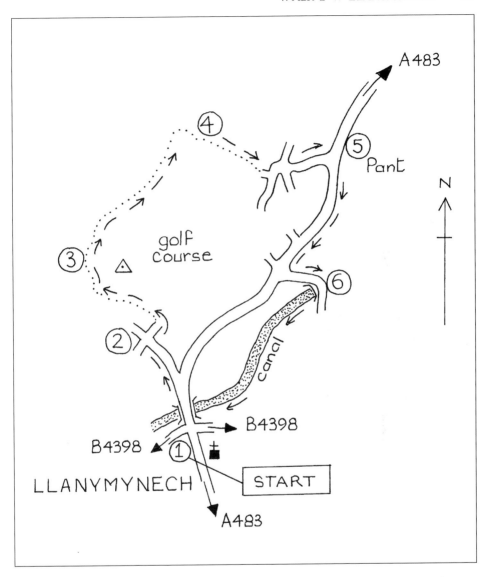

and carts had been used to transport the stone. Dominating the other end of the village is the church of St Agatha built of this same local limestone. The church has been unlucky enough to have suffered from a small earthquake as well as being hit by lightning in recent years. There is a choice of pubs, including the Dolphin and Cross Keys near the crossroads and a few yards along the main road heading south is the Lion Hotel. Near the car park is the post office and shop with tourist information.

The initial steep climb is rewarded by dramatic and ever-changing views, and

The international Lion Hotel

once up on the hill top, the flowers, birds and butterflies all add to the enjoyment of this walk. The return is partially on the road but ends with 1/2 mile along the canal towpath, another environment rich in wild life.

THE WALK

❶ Go over the stile at the end of the car park, turn right along the canal and at the road bridge turn left and walk away from the village centre. Fork left at the first turning off the main road, following the signposts to Pen y Foel and Offa's Dyke Path. Climb up this narrow road and note the steep limestone slope to the right, clothed with trees except on the highest near-vertical section.

❷ Just past the Pen y Foel cottages on the left, fork right at a minor crossroads. Climb up to the last house on the road, and a stile on the left of the driveway. Go over the stile and keep climbing, following the Offa's Dyke and the acorn signs. Reach another stile after a few yards, and follow the narrow path through trees. The path becomes horizontal and there is a left turn and then a steep climb. At a T junction in the path, turn left and go over a stile. When the path splits take the left fork. The hill is carved by

---

FOOD and DRINK

The Lion Hotel (telephone: 01691 830234) has two lounges, the front in Wales and the rear in England, and a boundary line between the two rooms, and countries, is marked on the wall. A variety of food is available at lunch times and in the evenings, as well as accommodation if required.

---

old limestone quarries, which also yielded lead, copper and zinc. Views open up to the left. Fork right at the next junction through an area rich in wild flowers including orchids – real limestone flora and fauna – with many insects, butterflies, dragonflies and birds. Keep straight on, at the foot of the large rocky outcrop of the Asterley Rocks and still following the acorn.

❸ Reach the end of the Montgomery Wildlife Trust Nature Reserve and go through the wooden gate on to the golf course. Turn left along the margin, but after 30 yards go left along the path into the undergrowth. Emerge on to the golf course again and turn left along the edge of the fairway, passing the 14th green. Just before reaching the 15th green, veer left off the fairway still following the Offa's Dyke path. Continue through the woods, then pass over a stile. At a T junction, where the Offa's Dyke path goes down left, turn right. The path soon splits but keep right (straight ahead really) and descend through the woods to a stile beyond which is the golf course again.

❹ Go straight across the 5th fairway, and to a grassy path leading through trees to reach the 4th fairway. Follow the arrow straight across the fairway to a large wooden post with footpath sign. At the marker post is a narrow path going downhill, descending steeply to a gate. Once through the gate, turn left for a few yards along the drive and then almost immediately left again along the narrow road. Follow this road downhill, ignoring turnings, to reach the main road, where you discover you have been walking along Tregarthen Lane.

❺ Turn right along the road (A483) to walk through the village of Pant. Once beyond the Cross Guns at the end of Briggs Lane, the road to the golf course, look for Rhiew Revel Lane. Turn left down here to the canal bridge, where you turn right.

❻ Go over a gate and turn left along the canal towpath. The canal is at present overgrown and a wonderful nature reserve. There are plans to clear this section to link the already navigable sections a few miles to the north and the south, to enable navigation to take place throughout the entire 35 miles from Oswestry to Welshpool again. Just before reaching Llanymynech, the tall brick tower in the Heritage Area stands out in the trees to the right.

> **PLACES of INTEREST**
>
> The **Llanymynech Heritage Area**, open at all times, shows evidence of the old lime processing works as well as the railway and the canal, both of which arose because of the limestone working. The chimney has been recently restored and there are old bottle kilns as well as the rare Hoffman Rotary Kiln.

A Cymru stile indicating the boundary with Wales

PONTESBURY

Length: 3¹/₂ miles

Getting there: Pontesbury stands on the A488, south-west of Shrewsbury.	**Parking:** There is a limited amount of roadside parking. **Maps:** OS Landranger 126	Shrewsbury and surrounding area, or OS Pathfinder 889 Dorrington and Cressage (GR 406061).

The old part of Pontesbury is dominated by the church of St George which stands on a large island with one-way roads on either side. The large tower of this mainly 19th century church is sandstone, and in the churchyard, just outside the church door, is a sun dial. The black and white house opposite the church is one of several attractive buildings in this former mining settlement. There is a selection of shops as well as several pubs in the village, and Pontesbury was the home of the Shropshire novelist, Mary Webb.

An unavoidable part of this circuit is the very steep ascent to an ancient hill fort, but it is worth every breath for the quite

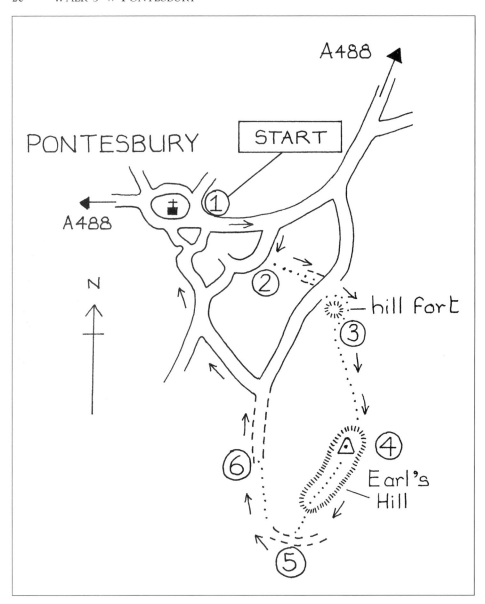

outstanding 180 degree views from the top, taking in Long Mynd and Caer Caradoc on one side, and the Stiperstones and the hills of Wales on the other. The return route is through Earl's Hill Nature Reserve.

THE WALK

❶ From the church, walk along the road towards Shrewsbury, passing the Red Lion and the narrow road to Habberley. The Public Hall is also on the right, and shortly

The summit of Pontesbury Hill

beyond this reach the right turn to Mary Webb School (and Pontesbury Further Education Centre). Turn along this lane, with playing fields on the left, and then the school on the right, to the point where the road divides. Here turn left, along a narrow lane. Pass a second playing field on the left, and the narrow lane then climbs a little.

FOOD and DRINK

There are several pubs in the village. The Red Lion (telephone: 01743 790321) is located quite close to the church, and offers a good choice of home-cooked food at the bar.

---

❷ After the climb, look for a small stile on the left. Go diagonally across the field to reach a stony track where you turn left. The stony track leads to a cattle grid and then a narrow road. Turn right, and after a few yards of climbing, reach a Forestry Commission car park on the left. Go into this and leave from the left side along a broad stony track which bends round to the right. The track narrows to a broad path and climbs steadily through the trees, a mixed assortment of deciduous, with a few tall conifers. Keep climbing and bending slightly to the right to reach a nearly level stretch. On the left is a footpath (where you will turn) but first continue for a few more yards to reach an open grassy area on the right, from where good views can be enjoyed. An old hill fort stands at the northern end of this hill, and like the fort on the top of Earl's Hill which you are about to ascend, dates back to 600 BC.

❸ Retrace a few yards to the path seen earlier, which begins as a narrow rainwash gully, and go steeply up Pontesford Hill. This steep ascent soon leads into an area of coniferous trees, although there is plenty of lower growth, with rose bay willow herb, ferns, brambles, and elder. Reach a few yards of a more gentle incline, before a steep stretch on to a small grassy open area. Beyond this the path leads into more trees, and is gentler, soon reaching a stile, fence, and the edge of the woods.

❹ Go on up towards the summit of Earl's Hill, across a grassy area, some bracken and a few trees. Note the lone hawthorn near the summit, where the triangulation point is at 1,050 feet. The views are impressive, including the two man-made structures of the Shelton Water tower to the north-east and the tall chimney at the Eden Valley factory at Minsterley to the south-west. The most prominent hills include the Wrekin to the east, Caer Caradoc to the south-east and the Stiperstones to the south-west. Keep straight on towards the southern end of the hill, passing the rim of the hill fort just before the steep descent begins. Over to the right can be seen the imposing church tower in the centre of Pontesbury. Go on steeply down to the woods, passing a few small hawthorns, to reach a stile and then a T junction at a major path.

PLACES of INTEREST

South of Pontesbury, just off the A488, is the small village of **Snailbeach**, famous for mining as long ago as Roman times and now the site of an excellent mining museum – you can take the self-guided tour.

---

❺ Turn right here. The woods slope steeply on the right, and to your left is a wire fence with woods going on down beyond. Before reaching the bottom of the slope, turn right along a fairly horizontal clear path marked with a blue arrow, and continue through the woods. This path begins to descend and drops to a stile and a major path.

❻ To the right the path leads up Craft Valley, but turn left to a notice board with information about the Earl's Hill Nature Reserve, which is a Site of Special Scientific Interest and covers an area of 105 acres. The hill was formed by volcanic activity over 600 million years ago. Go through the kissing gate and after about 20 yards at the broad track turn right to head back towards Pontesbury. Walk along the track and pass a house, after which the drive becomes surfaced and you reach more houses and a road junction. Keep left here along the country lane lined with high banks and hedges, passing more houses, and the church tower soon comes into view. At the end of Grove Lane, turn right and soon reach a ford on the left, and the adjacent Plough Inn. Just follow the road back towards the church and the centre of the village.

BISHOP'S CASTLE

Length: 4 miles

Getting there: Bishop's Castle is on the A488 between Knighton and Shrewsbury, or along the A489 west from Craven Arms. Parking: The main car park is	at the bottom of the hill, on Harley Jenkins Street, and another car park is available in the Auction Yard when there is no market taking place (livestock markets normally on Friday and Saturday).	Maps: Landranger 137 Ludlow, Wenlock Edge and surrounding area, or OS Pathfinder 930 Bishop's Castle and Clun (GR 323887).

Although today having no bishop and practically no castle, Bishop's Castle has the buildings of an ancient settlement with the charm of a rural location, set in the midst of unspoilt hill country. At the top of the main street, the only remnants of the 12th century castle, built by the Bishops of Hereford, can be seen in the garden of the Castle Hotel. Also at the top end is the Three Tuns which brews its own beer in

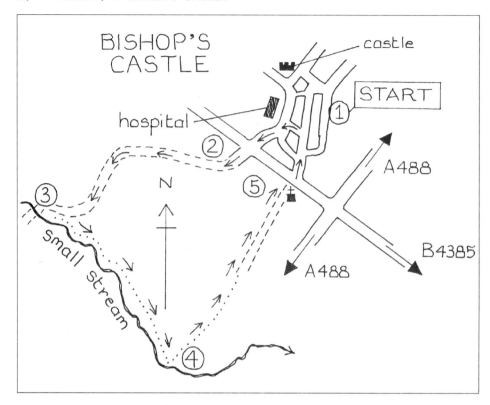

the adjacent brewery. The Town Hall with its clock tower dominates the High Street, and looks down on a collection of buildings dating from the 16th century onwards, including second-hand books, antiques and crafts shops to interest the visitor. Behind the Town Hall is the 16th century House on Crutches, one of three Tudor houses, now containing a museum of local history. Often very busy, Bishop's Castle is particularly popular on the second weekend in May for the May Fair, and the penultimate weekend in June for the Rush Bearing Festival.

This walk takes you on a pleasant circuit of the surrounding countryside, through green fields bright with wild flowers in spring and early summer. You follow the Shropshire Way by a little stream, before turning back towards Bishop's Castle.

FOOD and DRINK

Numerous excellent pubs and cafes are available, but we chose the Castle Hotel, a 300 year old stone building with some wooden shingles hanging on the back wall near the garden, from where the surrounding countryside can be seen and admired. Above the garden is a crown bowling green, one of the oldest in England. This old coaching inn serves home-cooked food, from an ample menu, with bar food as well as full scale meals to satisfy all tastes in pleasant and comfortable surroundings. Telephone: 01588 638403.

The House on Crutches

THE WALK

❶ If starting from the top of the 1 in 6 hill, walk down towards the church, and at Harley Jenkins Street turn right. Pass the car park (or start from here) and turn left for a few yards then right along Corporation Street. Reach a narrow road but go straight across along Woodbatch Road, and continue to the end of the houses.

❷ Walk out into the countryside along the narrow lane, and begin to climb gently between hedges and banks. The winding lane climbs and near the top are two paths going off to the right. Keep straight ahead, passing a new house on the left and the drive to Lower Woodbatch Farm, and barns, on the right. Views all around change with every bend, but dominant are the woods on most of the hills and rich, lush green fields on the lower ground. The narrow lane begins to descend and at the bottom, just before reaching the stream, turn left through an iron gate following the footpath sign and the buzzard logo of the Shropshire Way.

❸ The path leads through rich lush meadows along the valley bottom, with the stream a few yards to the right. Keep straight ahead through fields and over stiles to the point where the path goes right, on to a track, at a stile and gate.

❹ Do not turn right here, but turn left to go up the hill, a few yards away from the hedge, now on your right. At the top of the field, find the stile in the corner and go over and straight ahead, with a hedge on your right and a field sloping up to the left. Just keep going, through the next two fields, and the path becomes a track. At a gate,

---

PLACES of INTEREST

Five miles to the north is the remarkable rocky hill of **Stiperstones**, which features in local author Mary Webb's writing. The distinctive Stiperstones rock is quartzite, formed about 500 million years ago. The old mining settlement of Snailbeach is on the northern slopes of these hills.

---

the track bends left, but keep straight ahead between hedges, along a green lane. Beyond the flat plain down to the right is Oakeley Mynd with its mast and ahead and to the right is the western edge of Long Mynd. The path leads through to a stile and gate beyond which are the first houses (Field Cottage) and a stony track. When this track reaches a T junction, turn right for a few yards and then left along the narrow road.

❺ Pass the high wall, old barn and The Vicarage on the right, with the Fire Station to the left. Then reach the Old Vicarage next to the churchyard, with a rookery overhead, including some nests in the tall Scots pine trees. You are now at the bottom of Church Street, by the Six Bells, still with its own brewery, but stop to pay a visit to the parish church of St John the Baptist, passing through the lych gate of 1894. The first church on this site was in the 13th century and dating from that time are the old font and the archway in the garden wall of the Vicarage, opposite the west end of the church. The present church mostly dates from Victorian times. Enjoy a stroll around the other interesting buildings of Bishop's Castle before returning to your starting point.

CLUN

Length: 6 miles

Getting there: Clun is on the A488 between Knighton and Bishop's Castle, or along the B4368 from Craven Arms.

Parking: A large parking area

at the Clun Memorial Hall and Recreation Area is reached by turning up Hospital Lane by the Methodist church and passing the Holy Trinity Hospital, or by following

signs to the Youth Hostel.

Maps: OS Landranger 137 Ludlow, Wenlock Edge and surrounding area, or OS Pathfinder 930 Bishop's Castle and Clun (GR 302811).

This attractive village set in the midst of hilly countryside first grew on the south side of the River Clun, as a Saxon settlement near the church. St George's church has large yew trees outside the door, and although there are records of a

church here in the 11th century, the present building mostly dates from 1877. Interesting features include the lower part of the tower which is Norman, and a Norman arch behind the organ. At a later date the castle was built on a hill on the

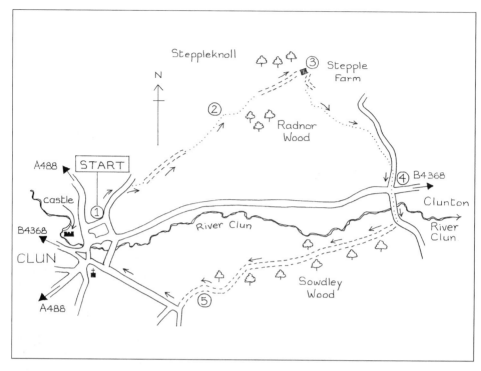

opposite side of the river, by Picot de Say who was one of William the Conqueror's followers. The original castle was of wood, surrounded by a moat and the river, and it controlled the valley route into Wales. A stone castle was built by the FitzAlan family and used from the 12th to the 16th century, after which it fell into disrepair. What can be seen today are all remnants of

the stone castle, and the main fragment is a large part of the great tower, built into the hillside. It is thought to have been used by Sir Walter Scott as the basis of the fortress in *The Betrothed*. Adjacent to the castle is the main part of Clun, a planned 12th century village, which now contains most of the housing and shops, as well as two pubs and a museum in the main square. Not to be missed is the Holy Trinity Hospital built in 1614 by Henry Howard, Earl of Northampton, and now almshouses with peaceful and attractive gardens.

Clun is set in the heart of green hills, and this walk takes you round two of the hills and across the beautiful Clun valley, with stunning views in all directions. You may even find a fossil! The return is along lovely woodland paths, rich in bird life.

FOOD and DRINK

The Buffalo (telephone: 01588 640225) is an old pub but immaculately maintained and offers an excellent choice of home-cooked food daily, at lunch time and in the evening. There is a selection of bar meals and also a restaurant. From the garden there are good views over Clun and the surrounding countryside.

Clun Castle

THE WALK

❶ From the car park turn left along the narrow road to walk past the Youth Hostel. Shortly beyond this look for the stile in the hedge to the right. Go over here and diagonally left to cross two fields to reach a gravelled track. Follow this track on a sunken lane between lines of trees, climbing steadily. Emerge into the open and keep straight ahead along field margins, passing a rocky outcrop where a few fossils might be found. At the end of the highest field, reach an iron gate and enter Radnor Wood.

❷ The path splits after a few yards. Fork left and descend along a clear path to a gate at the bottom of the woods where you turn right along the margin of the field. This leads to another iron gate beyond which you head diagonally left across the small stream and then up to a track along the bottom edge of the woods on Steppleknoll. Turn right here and follow the track to Stepple Farm.

❸ Go past the last barn and turn right, to follow a track. Go right through a gate, to follow the footpath sign. Walk down to bottom of the field and cross over the stream, then turn left. Walk through three fields and the path moves slightly left towards the stream, to reach a gate. Beyond the gate is a track, and when this crosses a ford to a gate, stay on the right side of the stream, and continue ahead along field margins. After two more fields head diagonally right across the next field towards the left of the large barns. Go through the gate and follow the farm drive leading round to the left and out on to the narrow road.

❹   Turn right here and walk to Clunton crossroads. Go straight on, passing the Crown Inn on the right. This narrow road crosses the river bridge. Just beyond Cwm Lane Cottage turn right through a gate and along the bridleway, which is a sunken lane and leads up to Sowdley Wood. Go through the gate and follow the orange arrow, straight on along the broad and fairly level track, for nearly 1¹/₂ miles. Pass through an open glade where a major track joins from the left. Occasional views open up to the right, down to the river and the road linking Clun and Clunton. Pass a track going down to the right, but keep straight ahead, and then move slightly further away from the edge of the woods. The wood has a fine selection of trees, with mixed areas as well as stands of conifers, but with areas of undergrowth too, so it is rich in bird life.

PLACES of INTEREST

The old Bronze Age hill fort at **Bury Ditches** on Sunny Hill is only 2 miles north of Clunton, and **Offa's Dyke** passes 3 miles west of Clun. This ditch and dyke once formed the England-Wales boundary, and is now followed by a long distance footpath, extending 177 miles from the Severn Estuary to the North Wales coast.

Notice some imposing redwood trees and then a few tall and magnificent firs, with very straight trunks. From here on there are several side tracks going off, but remain on the main track, bending round two small valleys going down to the right, and soon emerge from the woods between fields.

❺   Keep straight ahead and admire views opening out ahead to Clun and right to the Radnor Woods. The track leads out to a surfaced road. Turn right, and this leads back to Clun. Follow this road for just over ¹/₂ mile to reach the church and then turn right down to the medieval river bridge (where there is a small car park) and back to the starting point.

HOPESAY

Length: 4¹/₂ miles

Getting there: Turn off the A49 at Craven Arms, go west along the B4368 to Aston on Clun, then turn right for Hopesay.	**Parking:** The road in Hopesay is wide enough to allow some parking.	**Maps:** Landranger 137 Ludlow and Wenlock Edge, or OS Pathfinder 930 Bishop's Castle and Clun (GR 391833).

The tiny village of Hopesay is lovely, set in a valley surrounded by hills. It is difficult to find, but that may be more of an advantage than a complaint! Several attractive old houses are clustered along the narrow road, and on the road to the church are more houses including the magnificent Rectory. The church of St Mary also serves the village of Aston on Clun. Adjoining the church is a conservation area, in an old field which was formerly an area of neglected grassland, part of the rectory garden. It was reclaimed by local volunteers in 1988 – and is now

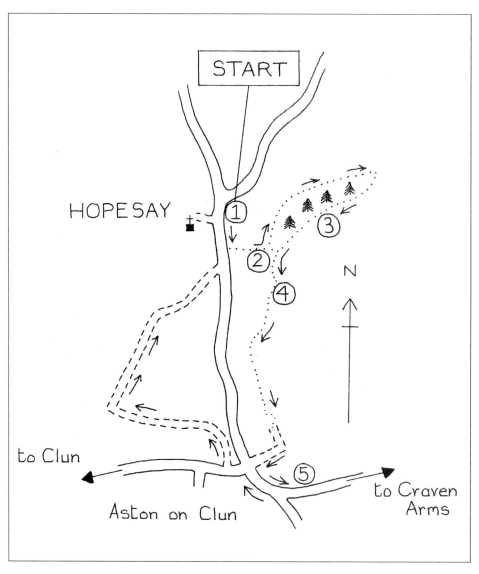

tended by the local school. In the church is
a wooden chest, perhaps the oldest in
Britain, dug out from a huge log. The iron
work and lock date from about 1200, but
the chest is almost certainly older. The
money slot on the top was cut in about
1160, possibly to collect contributions for

Richard the Lionheart and his Crusades.

For fine views across the valley, the walk
climbs to the top of Hopesay Hill. The
route from the hill is along the eastern
slopes of the valley down to Aston on
Clun, where you can seek out the Arbor
Tree, the two round houses and the

The decorated Arbor Tree in Aston

Kangaroo, before returning to Hopesay along the west side of the valley.

THE WALK

❶ Walk southwards along the road out of

FOOD and DRINK

The Kangaroo has been called by this name since at least 1820, and Australian memorabilia as well as local rhymes decorate the walls. A good selection of food is available at lunch time and in the evening, except on Tuesday. The menu includes Pam's Specials and there is a blackboard with daily specials too. Telephone: 01588 660263.

---

the village. (Beyond the last house, note a sunken track coming in from the right, as this is the route of your return at the end of the walk.) A few yards further along the road, turn left through an old iron kissing gate and cross the narrow field. Go on over the stream, across another small field and over a stile. Climb up to an old iron kissing gate at the top corner of the field.

❷ A few yards beyond this, turn left through a wooden gate, and follow the nearly level path along the left margin of the woods. You are now on the lower slopes of Hopesay Hill, an area of open land managed by the National Trust and used for sheep grazing. It is also frequented by buzzards. After passing through a few conifers near where a sunken track comes up from the left, go right up a diagonal path through the bracken which covers much of this slope. Climb steeply at first, and then the path begins to level off. Once on the top, turn sharp right on the grassy summit ridge.

❸ Walk on the broad grassy path, and pass to the left of the clump of conifers. There are now good views to left and right. Across to the west, beyond Hopesay village is the Iron Age fort on top of Burrow Hill. A valley is to the left as you descend quite steeply on the grassy path. The church clock down in Hopesay is likely to be heard chiming. Near the bottom of the slope, pass through the wooden gate again (2) and fork left down to the left of the house.

❹ Reach a stile and turn right along the driveway for a few yards, then go left through a gate and climb slightly. The path goes on over a stile and into a grassy field, and leads on southwards along the side of the valley, through several fields. Follow the yellow arrows on frequent marker posts, to reach a lone house on the left. Join its drive and descend into Aston on Clun. Go through a large iron gate and alongside houses. The road bends right, and you soon pass one of Aston's circular stone houses before reaching the Arbor Tree with its flags at the road junction. Decorating trees used to be a common occurrence, but the Arbor Tree dressing ceremony here in Aston is the last to survive in England. It has been decorated since 1786, when the local squire

---

PLACES of INTEREST

Stokesay Castle, perhaps the finest fortified manor house in England, is well worth a visit. It is open daily, in the care of English Heritage – see Walk 10 for more details.

John Marston married Mary Carter on 29th May. The present tree is a black poplar which replaced its predecessor in 1996. Turn left along the road for a short distance to visit the second circular house which is adjacent to the village shop and the pub, The Kangaroo.

❺ Retrace your steps through the village, to pass the Arbor Tree and several old stone houses including the old Post Office and Arbor Cottage, then Malthouse Cottage and the Old Malthouse. Just beyond this on the right is a stony track, your route ahead. To the right of this track is a small wood with a rookery, and then the Old Hall. After about 200 yards, at the cross tracks, turn left along the track between fields. Then go through a gate and along the edge of one field. At the end of the field go through a small wooden gate to a crossing point of four paths, and turn right here along a sunken track. Climb gradually between fields, and pass through a gate into a more open field, at the top of which is a large gate. Keep straight ahead along a hedged track, and then through a small wooden gate as the path continues between wire fences. A sunken track leads you down to the road, where you turn left and walk back into Hopesay.

LITTLE STRETTON

Length: 6¹/₂ miles

Getting there: Little Stretton is off the A49 between Shrewsbury and Ludlow, just south of Church Stretton. Parking: There are two pubs	in Little Stretton, and if eating at either it may be possible to obtain permission to leave a car in their car park. Otherwise park along the narrow lane near the ford, where the walk begins.	Maps: OS Landranger 137 Ludlow and Wenlock Edge, or OS Pathfinder 910 Church Stretton (GR 442919).

Situated 1 mile south of Church Stretton, Little Stretton is like a small sister settlement, but now thankfully bypassed by the A49. The village is a haven of peace, with many old houses each of which has a story to tell. The church, with its black and white exterior and thatched roof, is one of the most recent buildings, dating from 1903. It formerly had an iron roof, but this was found to be too noisy and was replaced. In the churchyard is a useful information board describing features of

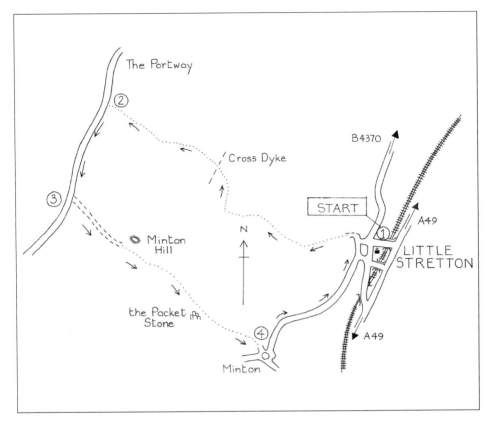

the village pre-1900 and post-1900. Opposite the church is the Ragleth Inn, formerly called the Sun Inn but renamed in 1905 when it became part of the Gibbon Estate. Also opposite the church is the Ancient

---

FOOD and DRINK

The village contains two pubs each providing meals and parking space. Both are highly recommended and I enjoyed the freshly cooked meal at the Green Dragon with its exposed oak beams and a very friendly welcome (telephone: 01694 722925). The menu choice is quite small, though with sufficient variety to satisfy all tastes, including vegetarians.

House, a 17th century posting house. On the left is the 15th century Manor House, home of the Gibbon family from 1701 to 1965. Notice on your right Darrell Cottage and Owls Cottage which were built as three cottages in the 17th century. In the early 19th century the three were occupied by a butcher, shoemaker and tailor, but by 1880 the tailor had taken over the entire building and was making riding habits for the London market. Also on the right is Tan House, which was a tannery in the 16th century, and on the left are Bircher Cottage and the Malt House, Bircher Cottage dating from about 1500 and the Malt House slightly older. Opposite The

The descent into Minton village

Stores is the Green Dragon dating from 1774.

The walk takes you out from the shelter of the valley to the open plateau of the Long Mynd, with a real feeling of moorland wilderness, where birds, plants and weather are very different from the lower land near the village. Joining the Portway briefly, a Bronze Age route along the Long Mynd, the walk returns by Minton Hill with views to the Clee and Malvern Hills.

THE WALK

❶ Leave Little Stretton via the narrow road alongside the Ragleth Inn. Just before reaching the ford notice Brook House on the right which was formerly a 15th century labourer's cottage, but has had several additions. Cross the ford and walk along the stone drive passing the camp site on the right and then the stone houses. Soon fork left across the stream. Follow the path through a gate and climb steeply uphill. The stream is now down to the right, as you climb, following the clear track. Near the head of the valley, the path bends to the left and then curves round slightly right to keep heading generally in a north-west direction. A steep valley is now to the left and all around can be seen bracken, heather, scattered hawthorn trees and hills. After a slight descent to a small col the path crosses an old boundary line, called Cross Dyke, and then climbs again on a very grassy path between expanses of heather. The path levels off as you approach a narrow road (at 1,558 feet), and leave the National Trust territory.

❷ To the right is the clump of trees around Pole Cottage, but turn left along the road following the route of the Portway, an old Bronze Age route. Notice the different land use on the right, when compared with the old traditional rough grazing of the land to the left. If this was not preserved as open heathland by the NT the wild landscape with the moorland plants as well as moorland birds such as red grouse would disappear. Walk along the road for about 1/2 mile and turn left where a marker post is located at the end of a track leading back on to the moorland, and eventually to Minton. Just further along the road, beyond this turning point, is the Midland Gliding Club.

❸ This track heads south-eastwards and climbs slightly to pass to the right of the top of Minton Hill (1,485 feet), from where the Clee Hills and Malvern Hills may be seen in the distance. After a fairly level stretch begin to descend, around the left side of a

PLACES of INTEREST

One mile to the north is the tourist centre of **Church Stretton**, and 2 miles to the south is the **Acton Scott Working Farm Museum** (see Walk 9 for more details).

very steep valley down to the right. Descend steadily, passing a rock to the right of the path. This is the Packet Stone, a vertical rock outcrop where packhorses were traditionally given a rest. Descend through the bracken to a field which narrows between two wire fences, as you pass an old quarry and reach the small village of Minton. Go through the gate and along the track to reach the village green – an unusual feature in Shropshire. Clustered around the green are two farms and several delightful stone houses.

❹ Leave from the left side of the green and follow the narrow country lane, which meanders between fields, back to Little Stretton. The Long Mynd is up to the left and Ragleth Hill across the main road to the right. Enter Little Stretton by Old Hall Farm, and then either turn left or right, depending on where the car has been parked.

CHURCH STRETTON

Length: 5¹/₂ miles

Getting there: The A49 and the main railway line pass through Church Stretton.	available in the centre of Church Stretton (pay and display).	Ludlow, Wenlock Edge and surrounding area, or OS Pathfinder 910 Church Stretton (GR 454937).
Parking: Parking space is	**Maps:** OS Landranger 137	

Described as an Historic Market Town, Church Stretton has the features and charm of an ancient village. It became a fashionable spa resort at the end of the 19th century and has plenty of amenities to serve the surrounding area as well as large numbers of tourists. The buildings are an attractive assortment of ages and of materials and several are of stone or half-timbered. An old barn has been converted into a smart Pottery, and at the southern end of the main street is the black and white Tudor Cottage probably built in the 16th century. The Tourist Information

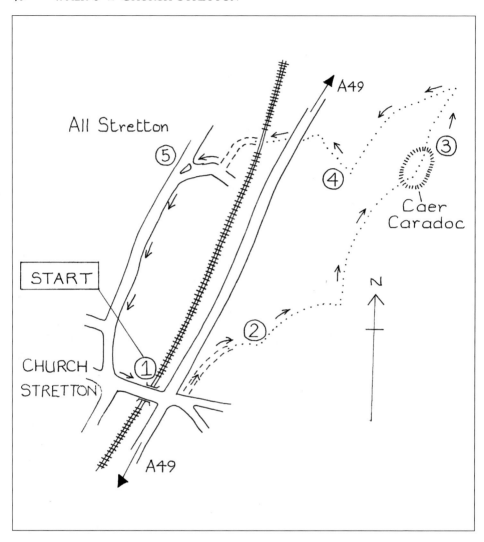

Centre is along Church Street, adjacent to the library and quite close to the cruciform church of St Laurence. Although originally a Saxon foundation, the Norman nave is now the oldest part of the church, which is built of stone, some ashlar as well as irregular pieces. Much of the church was rebuilt in the 1860s. Amongst the many other attractions in Church Stretton are several pubs and cafes, as well as the Fudge Shop and several antiques shops. Church Stretton is in the heart of Mary Webb country, and is referred to as Shepwardine in her books.

The walk gives you the opportunity to enjoy to the full the wonderful countryside in which Church Stretton is situated. From the slopes of Caer Caradoc, ever widening

The church's Norman north door at Church Stretton

and increasing views open up during the ascent to the ridge top, and from the summit they are incomparable – ample reward for the effort involved! The return is through All Stretton, another attractive village.

THE WALK

❶ From the centre of Church Stretton walk towards the station, over the bridge and straight across the main road (A49). Take the first road on the left, Watling Street North, and after crossing a stream, when the narrow road bends right as Helmeth Road, turn left along a narrow sunken lane. There are a few houses on the right at first, and an open field on the left, and the rocky top of Caer Caradoc is straight ahead.

❷ When this lane splits, and a Private Road to New House Farm is straight ahead, two paths go right. Take the second of these, over a stile to walk along the right margin of a field, with an old drovers' route in the sunken holloway to your right. Follow this field boundary which bends round to the left, and at the end of the field the path leads on to a track. Walk through a large metal gate or over the stile alongside, and

head into the woods. Fork left off the track to cross the stream at a small wooden bridge. As this path climbs slightly and bends towards the left, go up the steep slope through small hawthorn trees and then gorse, to emerge on the open hillside. Head towards the big rocks at the top, and reach a stile over a fence. Paths go right and left at this stile, but keep straight ahead to the top of the hill. At what appears to be the top, it is soon realised that more climbing is necessary to reach the highest point of Caer Caradoc, at a height of 1,506 feet.

FOOD and DRINK

A good choice is available of pubs, hotels and tea shops. The Bucks Head (telephone: 01694 722898) is popular with locals as well as visitors. A set menu gives a good choice of large meals as well as smaller snacks, and specials of the day, which is what I tried, with complete satisfaction. The Bucks Head has a garden and families are welcome. B and B is also on offer here.

❸ At the summit the all-round views are incomparable, and Iron Age inhabitants appreciated this fact by creating a hill fort which can still be seen today. The hills to the west are the Long Mynd and because of their geological composition, these summits are much smoother than the hills to the east which are all of volcanic origin. Keep straight ahead for the descent, which is very steep at first, but then levels off. Where there is a gate on the right, and a small pond ahead, turn left on a clear track which descends down the hillside. At the bottom of the slope, turn left to walk along the hedge and wire fence.

❹ When the path splits, take the right fork to reach a stile. Turn right and walk across a small field to another stile. Keep ahead along the margin of the next field, to a woodland area. Follow the wide track downhill into an open field and then across the main road, and straight on to reach the railway. Take care crossing the line and go left across the next field to a track. Turn right here and follow this to a road. Turn right to walk into All Stretton. The road splits and here you can take the right fork to walk into All Stretton village, or the left if wishing to return to the starting point as quickly as possible.

❺ Whichever route is chosen, when reaching the major road walk on the pavement to return to Church Stretton. Away to the left can be seen the rugged volcanic rocks of Caer Caradoc ridge which were created about 800 million years ago.

Looking up to Caer Caradoc.

ACTON SCOTT

Length: 3¹/₂ miles

Getting there: From the A49 3 miles south of Church Stretton, take the minor road heading eastwards to Acton Scott.	Parking: In the car park of the Working Farm. (Alternative locations on the route of the walk are on the roadside in the village, or at the village church car park.)	Maps: OS Landranger 137 Ludlow, Wenlock Edge and surrounding area, or OS Pathfinder 931 Craven Arms (GR 457898).

This tiny village is merely a few houses near the church and the manorial hall, with its neighbouring farm which is now the famous Historic Working Farm and Museum. The Tudor Acton Hall was built by the Acton family and dates from the 16th century. This brick-built gabled house, with mullioned and transomed windows, stands impressively overlooking the farm and the surrounding countryside. One of the drives from the house leads to a gate directly opposite the parish church of

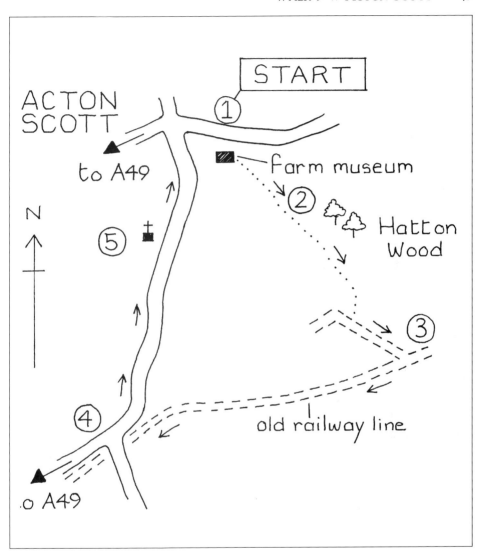

St Margaret. Built of local limestone, the oldest part of the church is the tower dating from 1291. Most interesting inside the church are the pews of 1896, and the three hatchments, one on each side of the organ case and one over the pulpit. These show the heraldic achievements of the deceased, a tradition of the 17th, 18th and early 19th centuries. The hatchment to the left of the organ case is of John Stackhouse who died in 1819, and to the right is that of his wife Susanna who died in 1828. Over the pulpit is their son's, Thomas Pendarves Stackhouse. The white background on the men's hatchments indicates they died before their wives. It was a daughter of

Old implements on display at the Working Farm Museum

Lord Acton who married a Stackhouse and hence the appearance of this name in the

---

FOOD and DRINK

The cafe/restaurant in the Working Farm is located in the old school, a mock Tudor building which dates from 1866. It took up to 60 children, some of whom had to walk up to 4 miles each way to school. It offers a set menu as well as a daily special and all the food is home-made and quite imaginative. Snacks are available all day and the cakes are an additional attraction and an excuse for overeating. Telephone: 01694 781306 or 781307. The nearest food otherwise is at Station Inn at Marshbrook on the A49.

---

village. The brass memorial on the chancel wall is for Elizabeth Mytton (died 1571) and her family of two daughters and nine sons all of whom are remembered on the brass.

The village is encircled by hills which remain in sight throughout this walk through an area of great rural charm, with views across to Wenlock Edge and Long Mynd. Part of the route follows the old Craven Arms to Wenlock railway, and begins by passing the site of a Roman villa.

THE WALK

❶ Leave the Working Farm over the narrow wooden stile in the corner of the car park, and head diagonally across to the far right corner of the field. In the middle of this field is the site of a Roman villa, discovered in 1817 and excavated in 1844. It was found to contain an underground chamber with tiles, pottery and bones, as well as some Greek coins. There had been nine or ten rooms in the villa and possibly baths. In the far corner of the field is a wooden stile, beyond which the path stays close to a hedge on the left as it winds through trees and undergrowth. At a T junction turn left about 20 yards to a wooden stile, and once over this, turn right along the field margin.

❷   Once past the trees, a view to the right will open out, as you walk towards Hatton Wood at the end of this field. Go over the stile and take the right fork when the path splits. Head across the field, slightly uphill, to a stile and then slightly right across the middle of the next large field, with its scattered trees. Keep going in the direction of the yellow arrow, but before reaching the overhead electricity wires, look for the stile on the right. Go over this on to a grassy track between fences and turn left.

❸   At the end of this track, reach the route of the old Craven Arms to Wenlock railway which operated from the 1850s for about 100 years. It has become a mini nature reserve, and you follow it for just under a mile, beneath the electricity wires again, then over a bridge, through a small wood to reach a road bridge. Walk on beneath a bridge. After 20 yards, although

---

PLACES of INTEREST

The **Working Farm** was originally the farm for the Acton Scott Estate, and in 1975 was established as a Historic Working Farm, to use the methods and traditions of South Shropshire farming as it would have been in Victorian times. It is open from April to October, Tuesday to Sunday and on Bank Holidays, from 10 am till 5 pm (telephone: 01694 781306). Other nearby attractions include **Stokesay Castle** just south of Craven Arms, or the **Nature Trail** near the church in Church Stretton.

---

the track goes straight ahead, turn right, to reach a gate and the road.

❹   Turn right along this road (Henley Lane), ignoring the right turn after a few yards, and keep ahead for nearly a mile back to the village of Acton Scott. The narrow road is between hedges and banks with views to Wenlock Edge over to the right and Long Mynd to the left. Pass a small stone house on the right and on the left is Wood Acton House. Next on the right is a small house, a lodge for the estate of the Hall. Then climb gently and reach a stony car park on the right, with Church Farm and then the church on the left, with its ancient yew trees.

❺   After visiting the church, continue along the road, to where the Old Rectory and farm pond can be seen on the left of the road, opposite the buildings of the Farm and the Hall. Walk straight on and slightly uphill to the crossroads, where you turn right to your starting point at the Working Farm.

CRAVEN ARMS

Length: 3½ miles

Getting there: Craven Arms is on the A49 between Ludlow and Church Stretton, where the B4368 Much Wenlock to Clun road crosses.

Parking: There is a free parking area in Craven Arms.

Maps: OS Landranger 137 Ludlow and Wenlock Edge, or OS Pathfinder 931 Craven Arms (GR 435828).

By no means a typical village, Craven Arms is a bustling and busy market centre, on main roads and railway and catering for a large rural area. Planned by the Earl of Craven to be a town with a grid pattern of streets, it never quite achieved the scale he had hoped. Yet, set in such beautiful surroundings, with hills visible in all directions, it is an excellent centre for walking in the magnificent countryside, easily accessible by road or rail. It is close to Stokesay, one of the real gems of the

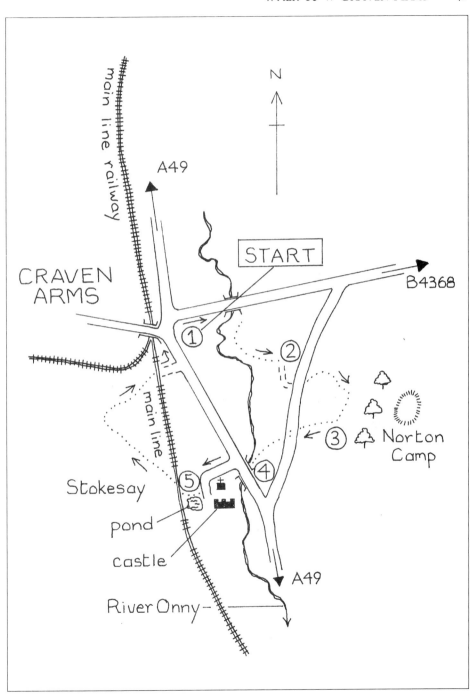

county. Craven Arms was developed at the expense of Stokesay, after the arrival of the railway in the 1840s. Before that time, only a tiny settlement had existed here, on the drovers' route from mid Wales. The most noteworthy building is the Craven Arms Hotel after which the village was named, and across the road is the cattle market which is still used on Wednesdays.

This lovely walk begins by climbing up towards Norton Camp on the nearest hill, with fine views overlooking Craven Arms, and then descends to recross the River Onny and the main road to reach Stokesay and its magnificent castle, before returning across farmland.

THE WALK

❶ Leave the car park and walk along the B road towards Much Wenlock. Once across the River Onny, turn right over a stile to follow the river, as far as a white footbridge. Do not cross the river but turn left, and head across the field to a small footbridge. Go straight on beyond here, up a short steep slope by a fenced area of trees, and turn right and then left, following the field boundary. In the far right corner of

---

FOOD and DRINK

From the choice of several eating places in the village, we were well satisfied with the Craven Arms Hotel (telephone: 01588 673331), an impressive old building dating from the early 19th century and which signified the beginning of the market settlement of Craven Arms. A fixed menu of bar snacks, with full meals and a daily special on the blackboard, provide ample choice. Well cooked food is served in a friendly and welcoming atmosphere, and accommodation is available if required.

---

this field, a track leads out to the road where you turn left. This is Whettleton, with a large stone farm complex and barns surrounding a courtyard.

❷ About 150 yards along this road, turn right over a stile by an iron gate. Bend slightly right and walk straight across the field. At the top of this field, go over a stile and climb more steeply alongside the field boundary. Notice the fine views over Craven Arms, with the main road and two railway lines. The single track line coming into Craven Arms from the west is part of the Heart of Wales (Shrewsbury to Swansea) line. Reach the bottom edge of Norton Camp Wood, which you enter over steps and a stile, and turn right to skirt along the bottom edge of the woods. The trees are mainly deciduous, with many beech and oak and sweet chestnut. Pheasants and other birds, as well as wild flowers are numerous.

❸ After about 200 yards the path turns right, out of the woods and downhill, following the sunken track down to the road. Turn left along the road, and after 100 yards go right over a stile and diagonally across the field towards a stile. Continue towards the river bank round an old abandoned meander, to a stile. Then cross the next short section of field to the steps, up on to the old road.

❹ Turn left here for 200 yards and walk out to the main road, where you turn right. Cross the river bridge and turn left to go to Stokesay, clearly visible to the left. The cast iron bridge over the Onny is one of Telford's, and dates from 1823.

The old milestone in the village

Pass the old Stokesay school, and then walk on to the church and castle. Just before reaching the lych gate notice the old mounting stone on the right. After visiting church and castle (see Places of Interest), walk along the road passing the car park on the right and the castle on the left to reach a gate. Turn right for the onward route.

❺ Go through the gate, now following the signs for Wild Edric's Way (Edric, a Saxon thane, was a local hero and resistance fighter, who burned Shrewsbury in 1069 but was subsequently beaten by the Normans) and the Shropshire Way, with its logo of the buzzard. Pass to the right of the pond, and along the track beneath the railway line – it may be muddy here. Turn right to follow the railway line for a few yards and then follow the hedge. At the end of a long field, reach a gate and stile. After a further 150 yards turn right over a

stile. Follow the right margin to the far end of the field and turn right passing a gate and stile on to the track leading out to the main road. Turn left here to walk back to the centre of Craven Arms.

PLACES of INTEREST

Stokesay Castle is open daily, though with shorter hours in the winter months. It is not a true castle, but is a crenellated fortified medieval manor house, claiming to be the finest in England, and with a magnificent great hall and an even more magnificent Jacobean gate house (which is still occupied). Built in 1240, by the de Say family from Clun, the house was extended by Lawrence of Ludlow later in the 13th century. Last inhabited in 1728, the house deteriorated until restored by the Allcroft family in the 19th century. It is now in the hands of English Heritage (telephone: 01588 672544). Next door to the Manor is St John the Baptist's. It was damaged in the Civil War, but was actually rebuilt in Cromwell's time – a very unusual occurrence.

BROMFIELD

Length: 4¹/₂ miles

Getting there: Bromfield is 3 miles north of Ludlow on the A49, at the junction with the A4113 to Knighton.	**Parking:** There is space outside the church, but this should not be used at times of services, otherwise park along the road near the church.	**Maps:** OS Landranger 137 Ludlow, Wenlock Edge and surrounding area, or OS Pathfinder 951 Ludlow (GR 482768).

This village with a long history is thought to have gained its name from the large quantities of broom which used to grow in the area. It grew up at the confluence of the Rivers Onny and Teme, with the church and priory, the gems of the village, built on the narrow promontory of land between the two rivers. The Benedictine priory was founded in 1155 but was ruined after the dissolution of religious houses by Henry VIII. The priory originally was a quadrangular group of buildings, with

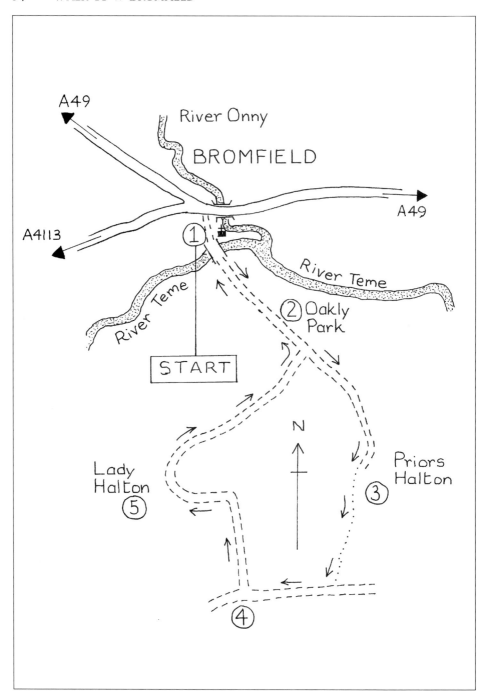

gardens to grow vegetables. The river provided fish, and the dovecote supplied winter meat. Little now remains, most notable being the beautiful restored Gate House, which is used as holiday accommodation. The church of St Mary the Virgin contains some remnants of the 11th century building, with the arches of the north and east walls of the chancel. The original tower was probably in the centre of the church, but the present tower was built about 1200. The church clock dates from 1887, and is a memorial to the Jubilee of Queen Victoria, who as a girl visited Oakly Park, home of the Earls of Plymouth. The row of oaks known as Duchess Walk was planted in her honour. The main part of the village alongside the A4113 has a variety of houses lining both sides of this road, and the old sandstone school building is now used by Pentabus charity. A more interesting collection of buildings is situated across the A49, with the post office and village shop, old cottages, the Cook House, and Bromfield farm. Further along the road beyond the farm is a large quarry, and in the field before reaching the railway line is the site of a Roman camp.

This is a lovely walk through an area of undulating Shropshire countryside and farmland – and there is no higher praise

than this. Crossing the River Teme, you enter Oakly Park and follow a driveway to the hamlet of Priors Halton, completing the circuit via Lady Halton and returning through the Park. The church, with an unusual memorial and painted ceiling, awaits you.

THE WALK

❶ From the large sandstone church, and the old priory, follow the driveway (Private Road notice) leading into Oakly Park. Cross over the River Teme, which has a weir and site of a mill close to the bridge, and pass to the right of the lodge. Parkland is all around, and the big house is to the left. Oak trees line the drive. The Earls of Plymouth owned the village as part of their estate and provided many of the villagers with employment.

❷ Pass the driveway going off to the right – this will be the route of your return journey. Keep straight on, through a gateway and down to a small stream and then up the other side of the valley, to reach the small hamlet of Priors Halton.

❸ Just beyond the last building, turn right off the surfaced driveway, over a stile and on to a mud and stone track. This track soon bends left and passes over a stream. Ignore the path going off to the right, but keep straight ahead alongside a fence on your right, with a stream about 45 yards away to your left. Climb steadily to reach a stile and a surfaced driveway, where the small wood on the left is called Woodcock Covert. Turn right along this narrow road and walk past a lone house which has commanding views out to the north. Look for a drive going off

---

FOOD and DRINK

The village shop sells snacks and ice cream and close by is the Cook House, formerly a pub called The Clive. It is open 7.30 am until 10 pm daily, with bar, cafe, snacks and a full menu for lunch or dinner. The delicious home-cooking in attractive modern decor is reminiscent of a smart city restaurant. Telephone: 01584 856565.

Scots pines in Bromfield churchyard

to the right, where you turn to head northwards.

❹ This leads to the isolated house Hill Halton where your straight route is blocked. Turn left to descend steeply to a stream, and then up the other side to the large complex of Lady Halton. Go through the gate. Turn right here to pass along the side of the large barns, and walk out to the main driveway through the park.

❺ Turn right and follow this driveway. Where it levels off after a slight climb, notice the avenue of trees on the left – Duchess Walk. Reach the T junction, where you walked on your outward journey, and turn left to retrace your steps to the church and the car park. Perhaps now is a good time to explore the church. The chancel was painted in 1672, but the ceiling is all that remains. It shows Biblical

> **PLACES of INTEREST**
>
> **Ludlow** is one of Britain's most interesting and attractive small towns, with a castle and numerous listed buildings, which can only be fully enjoyed by a gentle perambulation round the town.

texts and was financed by Richard Herbert of Oakly Park. A later addition in the church was the Hickman Memorial. Henry Hickman (1800–1830) spent much of his short working life researching into anaesthetics for painless surgery. He became a Member of the Royal College of Surgeons at 21. No one took much notice of him and others claimed the discovery about 20 years later. In 1930 a memorial tablet was unveiled in the church and some small recognition was given – belatedly.

CLEEHILL

Length: 4 miles (or 5 miles including a short circuit round the summit)

Getting there: Cleehill village is located along the A4117 between Kidderminster and Ludlow.	**Parking:** A large free car park is located at the eastern end of the village.	**Maps:** OS Landranger 138 Kidderminster and the Wyre Forest, or OS Pathfinder 951 Ludlow (GR 595754).

Straddling the A4117, Cleehill village cannot be described as pretty, but its location on the slopes of Titterstone Clee Hill is quite dramatic and gives rise to magnificent views – amongst the finest in England. It is the highest village in Shropshire (1,243 feet) and the second highest in England. One hundred yards from the car park is a toposcope (1,230 feet) which names many of the hills which can be seen looking towards the south across the plain. On the sloping common descending from the toposcope are mounds which are the relics of the former bell pit coal mines. A perambulation through the village will reveal an assorted selection of

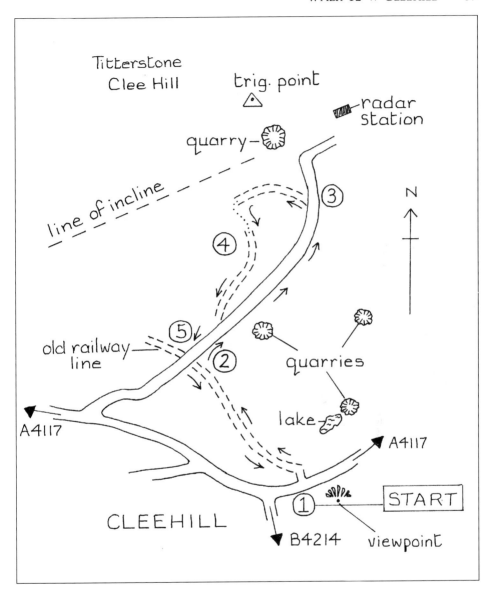

houses, which includes a few stone cottages, a village store, a post office (with information centre), a fish and chip shop and three pubs. Behind the village, Clee Hill slopes up to a height of 1,749 feet where the huge golf ball and dishes of the radar station can be seen from miles around. Clee Hill is the only hill in England which is marked on the Mappa Mundi in Hereford Cathedral, as it could be seen from there when Richard de Haldingham was compiling the map in the 14th century.

Looking across Clee Common with a dhustone wall in the foreground

It was already important at the time the map was made, because Iron Age folk built a fort on the hill top, and mining was well established by medieval times. The history of Clee is closely linked with the hill and its rocks, as mining and quarrying have been going on here for centuries, with coal, limestone, clay and iron, as well as the basalt known locally as dhustone, having had importance at different times. In recent years the work has been mainly associated with the extraction of rock for road gravel.

History and magnificent views are the main attractions of this walk, which takes you up Titterstone Clee Hill, and a treat is in store for any industrial archaeologist or ornithologist! The old quarries have turned part of the hill into an almost lunar landscape, with large areas of exposed rock, while elsewhere over the pasture

---

FOOD and DRINK

The Royal Oak is at the western end of the village, the Golden Cross is in the middle and at the eastern end nearest the car park is the Kremlin (telephone: 01584 890950). The Kremlin is the highest pub in Shropshire, and offers an excellent menu including home-made lasagne or curry, serving food at lunch time and in the evening.

and moorland birds from kestrels to sky-larks can be spotted.

THE WALK

❶ From the car park cross the road and go a few yards up the track towards the Kremlin public house. Turn left through an iron gate and walk along a clear track at the backs of houses. This leads between fences and areas of quarrying, now covered with grass. By a large quarry on the right, reach the remnant of buildings and follow the route of a former railway line, opened in 1862 to transport dhustone down the incline to Bitterley wharf.

❷ At the small hamlet of Dhustone, reach a minor road and turn right. A few yards past the last houses notice a gate and stile on the left, as this is the route of the return walk. Follow the very straight road for 1/2 mile. Around you can be seen rows of houses, built for the quarrymen or miners, and occasional isolated houses which were built on the land where squatters settled on the common, or where land was enclosed in the 18th and 19th centuries. Also across to the left can be seen the straight line of the Titterstone Incline built in 1887 to carry the rock down from the large quarries near the hill top. As you walk on, look around for some of the interesting bird life to be seen on this area of open moorland – buzzard, kestrel, raven, wheatear, linnet, curlew, skylark and pipit.

❸ The road bends left along a fairly level stretch, and just before it begins to climb

PLACES of INTEREST

The historical market town of **Ludlow** is only 5 miles away and is one of the few towns in Shropshire. The common all around Cleehill is open ground and it is possible to walk practically anywhere, discovering the rich bird life and wild flowers. Beware of the old quarry workings!

steeply, note the track going off to the left. This is your onward route, but before turning here, if the day is clear and some energy remains, you could continue up the road for about 1/2 mile to the triangulation point. At the top of the hill are the radar station and yet more old quarries, but views can be magnificent, over Shropshire and into Wales. The return walk follows the track, as it passes close to a group of buildings (Horseditch) and then bends left and begins to descend.

❹ Just before reaching a gate across the track, turn left down to a stream and a footbridge, with a Staffordshire Way symbol. Cross the stream and ascend slightly to the right, through the gate and along a field margin by a small stream (from one of the springs), to the buildings of Nine Springs Farm. Walk through the yard between the buildings and follow the track which leads back to the minor road.

❺ Turn right on the road. Shortly after the row of houses turn left to walk between a few more houses on your right and the route of the former railway on the left, and back to the starting point.

CLEOBURY MORTIMER

Length: 3¹/₂ miles

Getting there: Cleobury Mortimer lies along the A4117 between Kidderminster and Ludlow.	**Parking:** In the free car park behind the Talbot Hotel, a former coaching inn dating from about 1560.	**Maps:** OS Landranger 138 Kidderminster and Wyre Forest or OS Pathfinder 952 Wyre Forest and Cleobury Mortimer (GR 673758).

The curving and sloping main street of Cleobury Mortimer is lined with fine buildings, assorted shop fronts and pavements of different heights, but is dominated by the church with its crazy twisted spire of oak. The church of St Mary is of greenish sandstone and the oldest part is the tower which dates from 1160 – with a spire being added in the early 14th century. Much of the present church is from the restoration by Sir Gilbert Scott in 1872. The tower and spire were strengthened and restored in 1994. The famous east window commemorates William Langland (c1332–

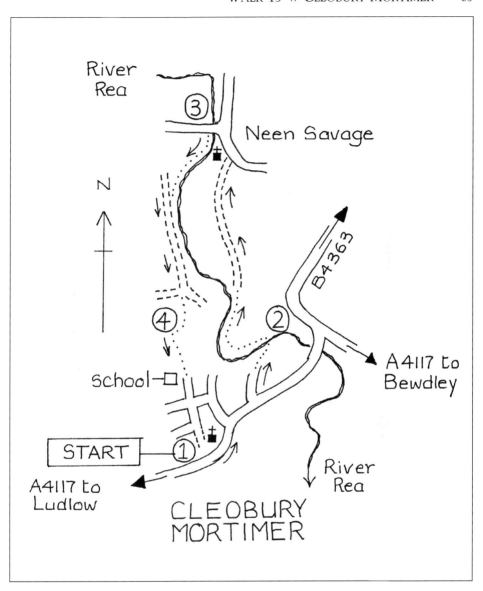

River
Rea

Neen Savage

③

N
↑

B4363

④   ②

A4117 to
Bewdley

School ─☐

START ─①

A4117 to
Ludlow

River
Rea

CLEOBURY
MORTIMER

1399) who is thought to have been born here, and shows Piers Plowman dreaming his dreams. Cleobury Mortimer was a Norman stronghold, and Baron Ralph de Mortemer (1086) built a castle here. It was later a noted small industrial centre, with mills and forges located in the Rea Valley.

This walk begins along the tree-lined (planted for Queen Victoria's Jubilee) High Street before following the tiny though steep Rea Valley through the heart of a rural landscape with more birds than people.

Approaching Neen Savage church

THE WALK

❶ From the Talbot Hotel, walk past the old Assembly Room building (about to be restored), and then the church, with the King's Arms opposite. Further along on the right is Wells Place (where the old well was once the local water supply), then the old

---

FOOD and DRINK

The King's Arms (telephone: 01299 270252) was a 15th century lodging and ale house, restored in the 18th century and now offering a wide range of delicious home-cooked food. An interesting King Henry VI sign hangs outside the main door

---

police station and a Methodist church. Pass a left turn, two more pubs and the Redfern Hotel, to reach New Road where you turn left. At the end of this road when it divides, take the right fork and keep ahead along the footpath going down to a small kissing gate and further on steeply down to a footbridge across the River Rea.

❷ Once across the bridge turn left over a stile and follow the river bank around the edge of a flat field, passing a small weir. This is where water was diverted for the paper mill, the remains of which may have been noticed just beyond the stile. A steep wooded slope extends up on the opposite side of the river. At the end of this field, go over a stile, passing Walfords Bridge on the left and a house (formerly another paper mill) on the right. Keep straight ahead along the track, with the river just on the left at first, and then it bends further away. As the track climbs, good views open up ahead. Approaching Neen Savage (Neen was the ancient name for the Rea), notice the black and white Lower Neen Farm to the right. The track leads on to join a road and you keep straight ahead, passing the Norman church of Neen Savage. Its tower formerly was topped by a wooden spire, which was burnt down in the 19th century after being hit by lightning. The road leads between the village hall on the left, and the vicarage on the right. The river is now alongside the route again as you follow this narrow road, to reach a ford, where you go left, over the footbridge.

❸   Once across the bridge and back on the road, go left over the stile and cross the field, between two large oak trees, with the river now to your left. At the end of this field go through a gate and along a small field to a stile and a path leading diagonally up the steep slope of the valley margin. At the top go over a stile, to a green track, and turn left through an iron gate. Walk straight along this track, between hedges. This leads to a gravelled track, but still keep straight ahead. Pass a house, Musbatch Farm, and follow the track to reach a narrow road. Go straight across here, over a stile and along the right margin of a field. At the end of the field, go right, over a stile and along the footpath passing in front of the buildings (Cleanlyseat Farm).

PLACES of INTEREST

Wyre Forest is the remnant of a much larger Royal Forest, and is noted for its very rich wild life, and woodland walks. The riverside walk as well as the Severn Valley Railway are on the eastern edge of the forest.

---

❹   The path leads down to a footbridge and beyond this you fork left alongside the fence to climb steeply up out of the valley. As the path levels off the houses of Cleobury Mortimer come into sight, and over to the right is a caravan park. The path leads between two gardens to a large iron gate. Go straight on, passing Cleobury Mortimer County Primary School and follow the road. Cross Langlands Road and keep straight on along a road to Childe Road and then a path which winds down to the churchyard. Pass to the right of the church and return to your starting point.

HIGHLEY

Length: 6 miles

| Getting there: Highley can be reached along the B4555 south of Bridgnorth. | Parking: In the public car park in the centre of the village (or a large car park on the road to Highley station). The walk starts on the main street. | Maps: OS Landranger 138 Kidderminster and the Wyre Forest, or OS Pathfinder 932 Highley (GR 742836). |

Highley is ablaze with colourful gardens and hanging baskets along the streets in the summer, and certainly does not give the appearance of the run-down old mining village which it must have been when coal mining ceased in 1969. It is now a busy small shopping centre with pubs, fish and chip shop, school and golf course. At the southern end of the main shopping area is the stone church of St Mary surrounded by its large graveyard, and beyond the church is the road to the

Highley station

Severn Valley Railway station and the Country Park, created in the 1980s. There are rows of old terraced brick houses typical of a mining village, but also much newer housing, especially in the northern exten-sion called Garden Village. Great restora-tion work has taken place not only in the village but also in the surrounding country-side where relics of mining have been replaced by green fields and woods. A few old remains of mining have been retained for historical reasons.

Highley is situated in the lovely Severn Valley and this walk takes you through wooded countryside to Hampton and then down to the river. The return is a relaxing riverside stroll.

THE WALK

❶   Walk along the main street, heading north. Just beyond a small Baptist chapel, opposite the open air swimming pool and play area, turn right along the narrow road to go gently downhill. When the lane splits, fork left along a stony drive, leading straight into Woodend farmyard. Go through here, passing two gates and veering left across a

---

FOOD and DRINK

The Unicorn is the focal point of Hampton and Hampton Loade, in a setting which looks idyllic on sunny summer days. A large amount of eating and drinking space overlooks the river. Open all day, the Unicorn offers a wide menu with snacks, bar food as well as larger meals. Telephone: 01746 861515.

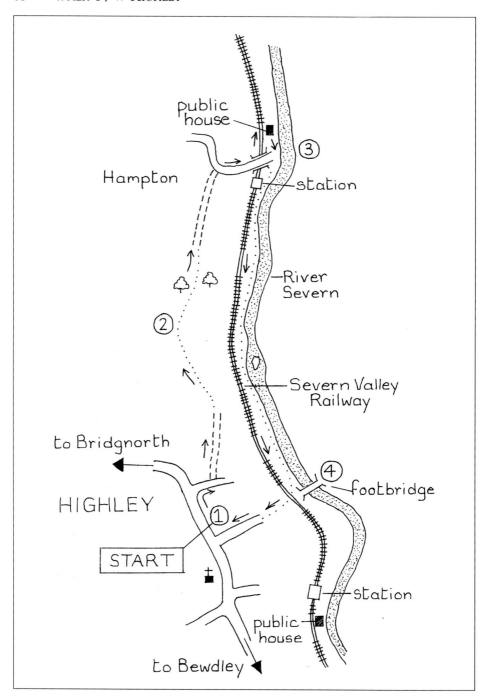

small field. Then go through a wooden gate and straight across a large field, following a Countryside blue arrow for a bridleway and also the Jack Mytton Way.

❷ In the far right corner of this field, go through a metal gate and along a track. When this bends left, keep straight ahead along the left margin of two fields, with the Severn Valley and the noise of steam trains down to the right. Pass through a small metal gate into the woods, still following the Jack Mytton sign and the blue arrow. Emerge from the woods and keep ahead between two hedges, along what has been a track but narrows to a path with summer growth of vegetation. Join a more open track but still keep straight ahead, and then descend towards the farm. Pass through a gate, the farmyard and two more gates to reach the narrow road. Turn right, and walk down the road passing the magnificent Hampton House and soon reach Hampton station. Up the lane to the left is the Unicorn Inn, but before going there for refreshments, walk on to the end of the road at the river bank, to see the unusual ferry, dependent on water power, which crosses over to Hampton Loade.

❸ From here turn to go downstream along the river bank, following the Severn Way sign with its trow logo (a type of boat used on the Severn). The path just follows the edge of the fields along the river bank, through meadows very rich in bird and insect life. You may catch occasional glimpses of steam trains on your right, on the edge of the woods which clothe the valley side. Fishing is under the control of Birmingham Anglers Association, and the

---

PLACES of INTEREST

The **Severn Valley Railway** delights old and young visitors alike. Open throughout the year, trains run frequently in the summer months, between Bridgnorth and Bewdley to Kidderminster. Telephone: 01299 403816.

---

banks are lined with fishermen's platforms and with trees in places. After passing the big house across the river, Severndale, and then the tree-covered island in mid stream, you soon reach a gate and stile. Just beyond these are steps leading off to the right, but keep ahead to the end of the Birmingham Anglers territory and arrive at the land of the picnic table and seats. This is the beginning of the Country Park.

❹ Pause at the overhead footbridge, which links the two parts of the Country Park on opposite sides of the river. You can if you wish walk on an extra mile to visit the History Trail, Highley station and the riverside pub, the Ship Inn. If making this extension, Highley village can then be reached by walking up the road away from the station and river valley. But if not continuing for this extension, turn right at the bridge and follow the sign to Highley, along a clear path climbing up through the woods. Cross over the railway into a car park area, with the private Severn Meadows Golf Club on the left. Walk from the parking area, passing caravans on the right, to reach a surfaced road, and just keep going along the road, climbing steadily. This leads on to the road between fairly modern houses and then a terraced row, to arrive at the main street. Turn right for a few yards back to the starting point.

MUCH WENLOCK

Length: 3½ miles

Getting there: Much Wenlock lies on the A458 from Bridgnorth to Shrewsbury, where it is joined by the A4169 from Telford, the B4378 from Craven Arms and the B4371	from Church Stretton. Parking: In car parks in Much Wenlock or a small National Trust car park on the B4371 (GR 613997) along the route of the walk.	Maps: OS Landranger 138 Kidderminster and the Wyre Forest area or OS Pathfinder 911 Bridgnorth and Much Wenlock, just extending on to 910 Church Stretton (GR 624998).

Large enough to be a small town, yet with many typical village characteristics, Much Wenlock is one of the gems of Shropshire. Its variety of building styles and ages depict many periods of the complex history of this fascinating market centre, and the stone and timber buildings lining the narrow streets preserve a medieval feeling. The Market Hall of 1878 houses the Tourist Information Centre and Museum, and opposite this is the black and white Guildhall, beyond which are Holy Trinity

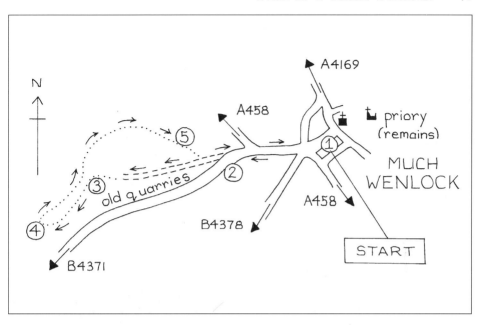

church and the Priory. The original church and the Priory both date from the 7th century but the existing nave of the present-day large Norman parish church was built by the Cluniac monks in about 1150 and the tower was added 60 years later. St Milburga, the first Abbess in the Priory, was buried beside the altar in the Lady Chapel, but her bones were moved to the Priory at the beginning of the 12th century. The surviving remnants of the Priory, described as monastic ruins set in an historic garden, are well worth a visit. The useful Information Board by the Priory car park, offers reminders of the local surgeon Dr Brooke who founded the Much Wenlock Olympic Society in 1850, and became actively involved in the early development of the modern Olympics.

Much Wenlock is not only a fascinating and attractive place in itself, but as this walk shows, the surrounding countryside is also magnificent. The ridge of Wenlock Edge is close at hand and a short circuit will give extensive views and take you along beautiful woodland paths.

FOOD and DRINK

Amongst several excellent eating places in Much Wenlock are the two pubs adjacent to the main car park. The Talbot Inn is highly recommended (telephone: 01952 727077), as is the George and Dragon which serves 'traditional country cuisine'. In the George we enjoyed a delicious lunch selected from a varied and imaginative menu. The choice includes bar snacks as well as full meals, and a special of the day on the blackboard. The George (telephone: 01952 727312) is a 15th century building, and the low beams have been decorated with a fine selection of jugs.

THE WALK

❶ Leave Much Wenlock along High Street, passing the 14th century Talbot

The local limestone is put to good use in the car park

Inn and the old Ashfield Hall and Raynald's Mansion. Turn right on the A458 towards Shrewsbury then left on the B4371. Just before reaching the Horse and Jockey fork right along Blakeway Hollow. This broad and well worn track on a sunken lane was formerly the main route from Much Wenlock to Shrewsbury.

❷ After a few hundred yards, pass the National Trust car park situated in an old quarry (an alternative starting point for the walk). Keep straight ahead along the track as it climbs steadily, between hedges and banks lined with flowers. After levelling off, just beyond a left bend, the track divides with the right fork signposted Harley Bank. Keep straight on, signposted to Blakeway Coppice.

❸ Go through the gate, following signs for the Shropshire Way, a circular long distance footpath of 170 miles, and Jack Mytton Way, named after Mad Jack Mytton who was born in 1796 at Halston Hall near Whittington. After about 100 yards go left along the narrow footpath towards Major's Leap. This leads you through a mass of wild garlic and out to the top of the woods, and along the edge of the old quarries. Look out for the log seat on the right. This is the Major's Leap, where the Royalist Major

Thomas Smallman from Wilderhope Manor is said to have escaped from his Parliamentarian pursuers by leaping over the edge. He survived, though it proved fatal to his horse.

❹ Shortly beyond this seat, turn away from the quarries and take the path going right over a large rock step and then steeply down the scarp, going left at first. Then turn right at a sharp elbow bend, to descend to the main track, where you turn right. Walk through the woods and back to the gate passed on the outward walk (3). Just beyond the gate, fork left towards Harley Bank. The track begins to descend and bends to the right, then levels off before descending further down the side of the scarp. When this track divides, take the right fork up a muddy track. When this splits take the stepped path going to the right. Reach a horizontal path but go straight on and up to the top of the woods and over a fence into a field.

PLACES of INTEREST

The Priory in Much Wenlock is a star attraction, and is open throughout the year (telephone: 01952 727466). The 16th century stone mansion **Benthall Hall** with its famous collections of paintings and ceramics is only 4 miles away. Now looked after by the NT it is open to visitors on Wednesday, Sunday and Bank Holiday afternoons throughout the summer (telephone: 01952 882159).

---

❺ Head across this hummocky field, to pass to the left of the stone barns (Stokes Barn, now a bunk barn complex, with stabling facilities). Once past the barns, bend right off the driveway to follow the field boundary to a wooden gate and then along the right side of the next field to a stile. Continue along the left side of the next field to another stile. Once over this turn left along the track, Blakeway Hollow, and retrace your steps to the starting point.

COALPORT

Length: 3 miles

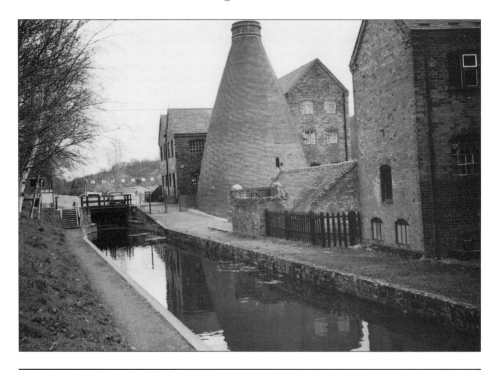

Getting there: From the A442 Bridgnorth to Telford road, turn left along a narrow road signposted to Coalport, about ¹/₂ mile north of the traffic island where the B4176 and B4379 meet the A442. Alternatively drive towards Telford and then follow the signposts to Ironbridge and thence to Coalport.

Parking: Use the Coalport Museum car park if visiting the museum, or the pub car parks (with permission) if taking refreshment, or park opposite the museum.

Map: OS Landranger 127 Stafford and Telford, or OS Pathfinder 890 Ironbridge and Telford South (GR 697024).

Time appears to have stood still in Coalport. The village is dominated by the bottle kilns and large buildings of the china works, the reason for the original growth of Coalport. The first houses in the village were built in the late 1790s, the Toll Cottage at the eastern (downstream) end and small cottages near the Tar Tunnel at

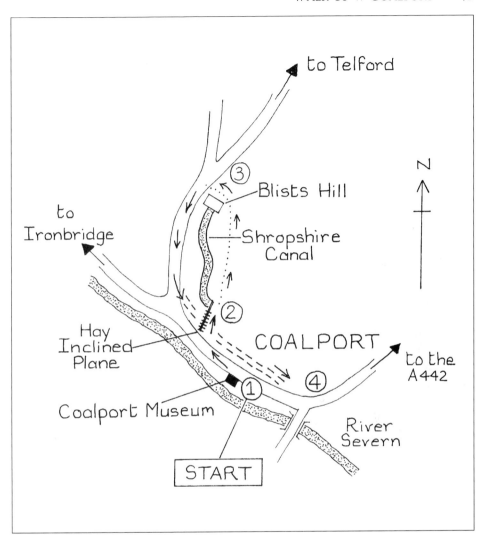

to Telford

N

Blists Hill

to
Ironbridge

Shropshire
Canal

③

②

Hay
Inclined
Plane

COALPORT

to the
A442

①

④

Coalport Museum

River
Severn

START

the western end being the first. Subsequently small houses were built near the factory for workers, although many of the employees lived across the river in Jackfield, and came over by ferry, or the footbridge. John Rose, who had been apprenticed at the Caughley Porcelain works, set up his own factory at Coalport in 1796, and the works remained here until they closed and moved to Stoke in 1926. They then became derelict but the Museums Trust has been able to restore them to reveal their fascinating history, and recapture the conditions of the workers in those days. From the china works a short length of canal leads to the foot of the Hay Inclined Plane, and formerly the canal extended further downstream to the wharf,

The iron wheel to be found on the Silkin Way

near the old bridge across the Severn, which though weakened is still usable by cars. Adjacent to this is the old Toll Cottage, and at the southern end of the village are two pubs with large car parks and garden space overlooking the river, an

---

FOOD and DRINK

Three excellent pubs in Coalport give ample choice of menu and all have parking space. Two of the three have riverside gardens and we lunched on home-cooked food at the Brewery Inn (telephone: 01952 581225), which was quite busy even on a weekday, a sign of a good reputation.

---

indication of the popularity of the village for visitors.

The wooded valley of the Severn is a very rural setting, yet contains the relics of the Industrial Revolution. You can discover how life must have been by visiting the museum and taking this circular walk up the valley side and around Blists Hill. With ample opportunities to use your imagination, you may picture the hard life of the 19th century, yet birds can be heard singing in the woods and wild flowers will be growing, giving a reminder that the industrial valley is surrounded by beautiful Shropshire countryside.

THE WALK

❶ From the car park at the museum walk alongside the canal and the bottle kilns to the Shakespeare Inn and the Tunnel Stores, behind which is the entrance to the Tar Tunnel. Adjacent to the Tar Tunnel is the bottom of the Hay Inclined Plane. The walk follows the Silkin Way, up through the car park alongside the Shakespeare, climbing a few wooden steps to a broad horizontal path which is the route of an old railway line. Where the path reaches this old track is an iron wheel, the symbol of the Silkin Way, which commemorates Lewis Silkin, the Rt Hon Lord Silkin, C.H. 'whose vision in his 1946 Act of Parliament founded the post-war new towns' – including the creation of Telford.

❷ Just before reaching a short tunnel beneath the Hay Inclined Plane, turn right up some wooden steps to climb a steep path. As the path levels off, note the remnants of an old building at the top of the Inclined Plane, where the steam engine was located for pulling tub boats up from the river to the canal. Follow the Shropshire Canal which can be seen to the left, inside the Blists Hill Museum, and this leads you through to the car park for Blists Hill.

❸ Turn left here and walk out to the road, Legges Way. Turn left along the pavement down the hill – this is still Silkin Way. Pass beneath two old bridges, an old

tunnel and follow the route of an old railway line again, down through the woods. Instead of turning right down to the Shakespeare, keep straight on, behind the houses to emerge at the road opposite the Brewery Inn. Your starting point is to the right, along the road, but first go left to follow the Silkin Way along the river-side as far as the old bridge (a cast iron bridge built in 1818 to replace the earlier wooden bridge of 1780) across the Severn, where the Woodbridge Inn is delightfully situated on the opposite river bank.

❹ Near this bridge is a new road bridge and also a new bridge (1995) over what was the old railway line heading on southwards to Bridgnorth. A commemorative panel states that this used bricks and coping stones from the original bridge over the former London and North Western Railway which was opened in 1861. Return to your car along the road at the museum.

IRONBRIDGE

Length: 5 miles

Getting there: Telford is easily reached along the M54, but is also accessible from the A5, A442 or A4169, and clear signposting will lead on to Ironbridge and the gorge.

Parking: Car parks are located in Ironbridge and free parking is found at the sites of several of the museums in the area. Payment is necessary to visit the museums but a passport ticket covers access to all the museums, and remains valid until all have been visited (however long that may take). The walk starts at the iron bridge, south side.

Maps: OS Landranger 127 Stafford and Telford, or OS Pathfinder 890 Ironbridge and Telford South (GR 674033).

Ironbridge is unique, a real one-off settlement, and has become a major tourist attraction during the last 25 years. The village is in a dramatic location clinging to the side of a steep gorge, cut by melting water after the Ice Age thousands of years ago. It achieved its world wide fame because of the ironmaking in the neigh-

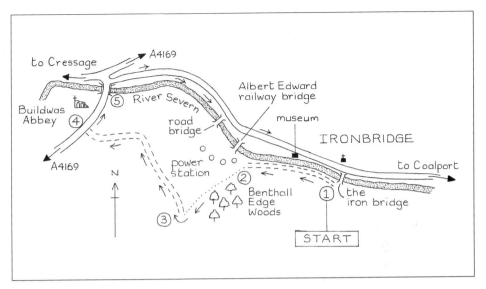

bouring area and the construction of the world's first iron bridge here in 1779 – 'a stupendous iron arch', and now a World Heritage Site. On the south side of the bridge is The Toll House, still with a list of charges, adjacent to which is the car park. On the north side of the bridge is the Tontine Hotel and behind this on the steep slopes of the gorge is St Luke's church built in 1837. A path leads up 120 steps to reach the church, but there is a gentler route up Church Hill. In addition to the Tourist Information Centre near the bridge, there is a Visitor Centre in the old Wharf about 400 yards upstream.

Leaving the famous bridge, we walk through the peaceful and ancient Benthall Edge Woods before reaching the tranquillity of the ruins of the Cistercian monastery at Buildwas. The return is a gentle stroll along the riverside path, with another historic bridge to admire.

THE WALK

❶ From the southern side of the bridge, follow the Shropshire Way along the route of the old Kidderminster to Shrewsbury railway line as it heads upstream and into the woods. The path approaches the huge cooling towers of the power station (374 feet in height, with the noise like a waterfall) and then you turn left.

FOOD and DRINK

Numerous pubs and restaurants are available in Ironbridge, but why not try the Tontine Hotel (telephone: 01952 432127) with rooms looking out on to the bridge. This old hotel dates from 1784, and like all tontines was built by a group of shareholders, in this case the same group of ironmasters who financed the iron bridge. The building is protected by preservation orders, though successful modernisation has taken place inside. Several old-fashioned features do remain in the hotel, note especially the Victorian tiled floor in the entrance, a product of Maw and Co of Jackfield. The comfortable lounge bar area has a wide ranging menu, including a blackboard with Today's Specials.

Ironbridge's famous landmark

❷   The path immediately splits and you turn left again, to climb up to a cross paths by a bench. Turn right, towards Benthall. Follow this path through the woods, as it climbs. When the path splits, take the right fork and climb steadily on a diagonal route across what is a very steep slope. The Benthall Edge Woods are very ancient and are rich in flowers and bird life. They were used as a source of charcoal in early iron working, and coal was dug from small pits by the monks of Buildwas as early as 1250.

❸   The path approaches the edge of the woods, and then joins a stony track coming up from the right. Turn left if you wish to walk on to Benthall Hall, but for the onward walk turn sharp right, and descend steeply out of the woods. The track soon bends left, and shortly there is another left bend and a Private Notice, but you go right here, over a stile and into an area of recent planting. The cooling towers dominate the view to the right, and between these industrial monsters is the green countryside which surrounds the Ironbridge gorge. The track leads on downhill through the Pool View Caravan site, past the coal mountain on the right, and out to reach the road, A4169.

❹ The onward route is to the right, but turn left for a few yards if interested in visiting Buildwas Abbey, which is situated in the riverside fields across the road. Now in the hands of English Heritage, these dramatic ruins include the major part of the church, though it has lost its roof. The church and cloisters were built in the 12th century for the Cistercian monks, who were still very active in the area in the 18th and 19th centuries.

❺ Turn right to cross over the river bridge and then right along the road leading back to Ironbridge, following the Severn Way with its logo of a Severn trow. Most of the return journey to Ironbridge is on riverside paths, but in two or three places, short distances will have to follow the road. The path leads past the magni-

---

PLACES of INTEREST

You can take a **boat trip** on the River Severn, or visit one or more of the **museums** at Coalport, Jackfield, Blists Hill or Coalbrookdale. It is at Coalbrookdale that the original Abraham Darby furnace can be seen. The central telephone number for all the Ironbridge museums is 01952 433522.

---

ficent old Albert Edward railway bridge, built in 1863 by the Coalbrookdale Company, designed by John Fowler who also designed the Forth Railway Bridge in Scotland. Just beyond this your path reaches the Ironbridge Rowing Club, the Dale End car park and the Visitor Centre and Museum of the River located at the Wharf, before the final few hundred yards into the centre of Ironbridge.

TONG

Length: 4 miles

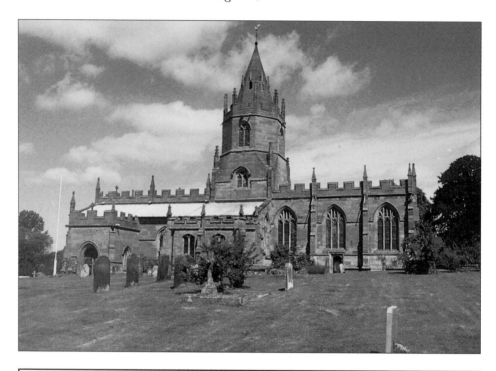

Getting there: Tong is just off the A41, only a few hundred yards from its junction with the M54.

Parking: Parking is possible in a layby on the A41 within sight of the church, or along

the roadside in the village. If eating at the Bell Inn, it is possible to leave a car here whilst walking, and in this case, to reach the church cross the main road, and walk along the minor road to the crossroads, then turn right.

Maps: OS Landranger 127 Stafford and Telford, or OS Pathfinder 890 Ironbridge and Telford south and 891 Wolverhampton (GR 797073).

The tiny village of Tong extends from the church along what is now a minor road, and is a haven of peace and tranquillity adjacent to busy roads. A small group of picturesque houses stand alongside the

superb perpendicular collegiate church of St Bartholomew, which was described in 1868 by the American consul Elihu Burritt, as 'a little Westminster'. It is certainly one of the county's outstanding buildings, and

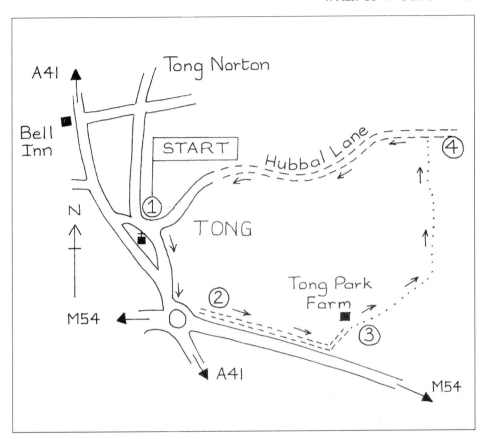

is noted for stone carvings, brasses and the Golden chapel added by Sir Henry Vernon in the 16th century. Some stones from the older collegiate church have been used in

the present church. Elizabeth, the widow of Sir Fulke de Pembrugge founded a college here in 1410, though the collegiate buildings to the south of the church have disappeared. Other features include several grand tombs including that of Elizabeth (also known as Isabel or Isabella), second wife of Sir Fulke de Pembrugge, who died in 1446. By tradition, a bunch of roses is placed in her hands every Midsummer's Day, the Feast of St John the Baptist. In the churchyard are some preaching steps, and close by is the supposed grave of Little Nell, the heroine of Charles Dickens' *The Old Curiosity Shop*, the final chapters of

---

FOOD and DRINK

A few hundred yards along the A41, food is available all day, every day at the Bell Inn (telephone: 01952 850210), a Milestone Tavern. It has an old sandstone obelisk milestone in the front car park, showing the distances to London, Salop and Wolverhampton. The large menu of meals and snacks often has a few blackboard specials as well as a children's menu. Sunday lunches are one of the specialities.

The old sandstone milepost in the pub's car park

which were set in Tong. Along the road from the church the village is divided on two short sections of road and every house is a gem, each for a different reason.

This lovely walk is set in the heart of the Shropshire countryside, in the fields and along lanes which make up the farming landscape, though horses are more important than crops in some of the fields. Wild flowers, birds and butterflies enrich the return route along Hubbal Lane.

THE WALK

❶ Start from the wonderful church and turn right at the churchyard gate. On the left is Friars Lane, leading to the old castle hill and also to and from the Bell Inn, then the black and white buildings of Church Farm and Holly Tree Cottage. Next on the left is the Old Post Office, of brick and sandstone, after which are the old alms-houses now four cottages, in a U shape round a courtyard lawn. Leave the village by passing the brick buildings of Tong House on the right, and Tong Hall on the left as you continue along what is now a country lane.

❷ When this narrow road bends right, to join the A41, go left along the concrete driveway towards Tong Park Farm. This is an area rich in bird life and bird song, with farm fields to the left and the narrow strip of woodland to the right. The concrete ends but keep straight ahead along the cinders, and when the drive bends left to the farm buildings, go more or less straight ahead, through a gate and along a grassy track. At the end of the field, reach a concrete track and turn left to walk away from the motorway towards the farm. Pass

---

PLACES of INTEREST

Boscobel House 3 miles away is where, fleeing from the victorious Roundheads at the Battle of Worcester, Charles II hid in an oak tree, before his flight to France. The house was built about 1600 by Charles Giffard. It is open daily from March to October, 10 am to 6 pm or dusk if earlier, and Wednesday to Sunday from November to March, 10 am to 4 pm (telephone: 01902 850244).

to the right of all the buildings.

❸ Once beyond the buildings the track splits. Fork right between fields, and at the end of the first field, turn left, to follow the hedge on your left. Stay by the hedge as it bends left and keep going ahead to reach a gate at the end of the field. Go through the gate, pass a small pond on the left, and the hedge is now on your right. At the end of the next field keep straight ahead, with no hedge to follow. Reach a small wood on the left, and a gate, and a T junction with a track.

❹ Turn left here and follow this track, leading you back towards the village. The track is lined by hedges and rough ground with many wild flowers, birds and butterflies. The track keeps more or less straight ahead to reach the buildings of Tong Hall Farm. Pass two houses on the right with shingled fronts, and descend into the village, passing an old sandstone quarry on the right. Then the Old School is on the right, followed by the Parish Hall, with the Old Post Office on the left. Finally on the right is Old Tong House (1465) with a wavy tile roof, before you arrive back at the church.

ATCHAM

Length: 4 miles

Getting there: Atcham is on the B4380 about 3 miles south-east of Shrewsbury, easily reached off the Shrewsbury Ring road.	Parking: Alongside the River Severn close to the church. The walk can be shortened by 1/2 mile by parking in the Attingham Park car park, although payment will be necessary unless you are a member of the National Trust.	Maps: OS Landranger 126 Shrewsbury and surrounding area: OS Pathfinder 889 Dorrington and Cressage, and 869 Shrewsbury (GR 542093).

This tiny village is steeped in history and located in a waterside setting alongside the longest river in the UK. The foundation of the church is Saxon and is the only church dedicated to St Eata, a Celtic saint who died in AD 685. Mainly dating from the 13th century, part of this red sandstone church consists of blocks from the old Roman city of Viroconium. The small window in the north wall to the left of the vicar's stall is Saxon in age, and notice on the stall the fine wooden carving of the

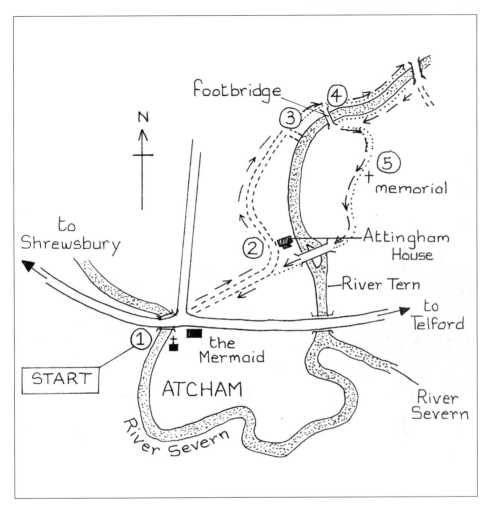

Parable of the Prodigal Son. A window in the north wall is of Tudor glass and contains a memorial to Blanche Parry, chief Lady in Waiting to Queen Elizabeth I.

The church is set alongside the River Severn, and the tiny village is clustered close by. On the main road are two bridges over the Severn. The present day bridge was opened on 24th October 1929, and the old bridge, now pedestrianised, was opened in 1776. The architect of the old bridge was John Gwynne, a founder member of the Royal Academy. Looking out to the road, bridges and church is the Mermaid Hotel, a listed manor house, with a crypt and access to the church via a secret tunnel. Originally a coaching inn, it became a private house in the 19th century. In the 1930s the house was bought by Sir Clough Williams Ellis, the architect who created the village of Portmeirion. He converted the manor house into a hotel

The two bridges over the Severn in Atcham

called the Mytton and Mermaid. The Mytton was dropped from the name in January 1997, just retaining the Mermaid, which is the crest of the Portmeirion Hotel. The walk is through the glorious grounds

of Attingham Park, an area of apparently traditional English countryside although it was created artificially by the efforts of Humphrey Repton. You cross open meadows and through woodlands, where snowdrops, bluebells and daffodils grow in abundance in the spring. The final section of the walk is through the deer park.

FOOD and DRINK

The red brick Georgian hotel, the Mermaid, offers accommodation and meals, and corporate entertainment as well as wedding receptions. Our more modest needs will be satisfied by the choice of snacks or full meals available daily in King Neptune's Bar. The Sunday lunch is particularly popular, and there is live music on Sunday night, with a dinner dance on Saturday nights. Telephone: 01743 761220.

THE WALK

❶ Cross the road from the Mermaid and go through Nash's gateway to the Park and walk along the drive. Over to the left is Attingham Home Farm, open to the public in summer, where several old traditional breeds are reared, in farm buildings dating from about 1800. The drive passes through a grazing area, where part of the village of Atcham was formerly located. Attingham is a neoclassical mansion, said by many to be Shropshire's finest house. It was designed by George Steuart in 1785 for the 1st Lord Berwick, whose son, the 2nd Lord Berwick commissioned Repton to design the Park. John Nash made alterations to the Hall in 1805–1807, including his famous Picture Gallery, the first roof-lit gallery, which used curved cast iron ribs from Coalbrookdale to support the window frames.

❷   Take the surfaced driveway to the left side of the buildings, and turn left to the Stable Block, now Regional HQ of English Nature. At the Stable Block, turn right along a driveway through tall trees, to pass the ancient Bee House, and the walled garden. At a large tree with a seat around it, fork left for the Deer Park Walk.

❸   The path becomes narrower and possibly muddier, and leads on round to a suspension bridge across the Tern.

❹   Just before the bridge, turn left over the stile to follow a permissive path alongside the river, for a delightful riverside walk. Continue through three fields until reaching the next bridge. There used to be a large forge and corn mill here, and the River Tern was navigable up to this point from the River Severn. Cross the river and retrace your steps on the other bank. On reaching the suspension bridge turn left to follow the clearly signposted Deer Park Walk, which is a broad track through the woods.

> **PLACES of INTEREST**
>
> The modern village of **Wroxeter** and the old Roman city of Viroconium are only 2 miles away, and **Shrewsbury** has a large number of attractions including a Brother Cadfael Trail, an abbey and a castle.

❺   Pass the memorial to Lord Berwick on the left and the path splits here, but keep straight ahead along the Deer Park Walk. Go through the large gate and follow the waymarked route to the left. Admire the parkland scene – hopefully with close sightings of the fallow deer, as well as sheep which may be grazing here too. When the woods bend left, turn right, still following the Deer Park Walk signs. Leave the deer park, cross the two bridges and then walk up slightly to return to the front of the house. To return to the Mermaid, retrace your route out of the Park.

GRINSHILL

Length: 3 miles

Getting there: Grinshill is situated 1 mile west of the A49 to the north of Shrewsbury.	**Parking:** There is a little roadside parking in the village, or along the lane leading to the church and the Parish Hall where the walk starts.	**Maps:** OS Landranger 126 Shrewsbury and surrounding area; OS Pathfinder 848 Wem and Myddle (GR 521235).

Grinshill lies at the foot of a steep and wooded hill. At the eastern end of the village are a few houses and the cricket pitch (Acton Reynald), as well as the Old Vicarage, opposite which is Stone Grange, a Jacobean house used by Shrewsbury School in the 17th century to enable scholars to escape from plague in the town. The main road through the village contains a few bungalows and houses of varying ages, all quite close to the Elephant and Castle. At the western end of the village is

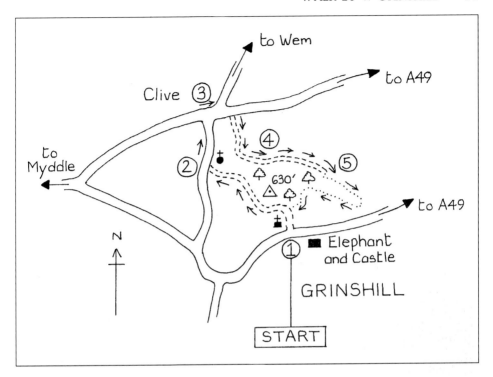

Grinshill Hall and just before reaching this is a lane to the right, signposted to the church and village hall. The red sandstone All Saints church dates mostly from 1839–1840, built in neo-Norman style and containing a little Norman masonry in two of the walls. In the churchyard is a sundial on the shaft of a medieval cross.

The walk is a double treat as the route takes you to the neighbouring village of Clive, where there is another interesting church, and back, as well as providing a spectacular hill-top view over much of Shropshire and into mid Wales.

THE WALK

❶ Walk along the lane passing the church, and at the village hall turn left along the sunken track, through trees at first, but then views open out to the left. The church is down to the left, but on the right is the steep wooded slope of The Cliff, up to the hill top.

❷ Just before reaching a narrow road, arrive at All Saints church in Clive. The church was rebuilt from 1885 to 1894, largely inside the Norman walls of the former nave. Two Norman doorways survive

---

FOOD and DRINK

The early Georgian hotel, the Elephant and Castle (telephone: 01939 220564) offers a wide range of food from bar snacks to full scale meals, in pleasant surroundings. Bed and Breakfast accommodation is also available. The hotel takes its name from the Elephant and Castle seen in the Arms of the Corbet family.

Grinshill's church

and the interior is noted for its wood carvings. An alabaster reredos is copied from Leonardo's *Last Supper*. The churchyard contains the grave of the 17th century dramatist William Wycherley, perhaps best known for *The Country Wife*. Your route is to turn right and walk along the road, passing the lych gate alongside which is the broad path you will be joining later. Just beyond the lych gate is Clive Court with an interesting barn alongside.

❸   At the T junction, a left turn would lead to the centre of the village, beyond the farm and large barn, alongside which is some parking space. However, for the onward walk turn right, and keep straight ahead to just beyond the signpost warning of a school ahead. Turn right along the Private Drive to Cross Trees (and public footpath). When the drive forks left, walk straight on along the grassy margin of a field and through a narrow alley to join the track coming up from the lych gate.

❹   Turn left to walk past the school on your left. On the right is a seat positioned to admire the view through a gap in the trees, looking south and south-west towards Breidden Hill. Pass a few stone houses and on the right are the woods which clothe this hill. If you wish to make the detour, there is a track to the right which leads to the summit (630 feet), with a toposcope and a spectacular almost aerial view down to Grinshill. More distant views stretch to Wenlock Edge, Long Mynd, Caer Caradoc, and over to the right is Cader Idris. Back on the path, reach a lone house on the left and pass another track that goes off to the right and meanders up to the trig point.

PLACES of INTEREST

Hawkestone Park near Weston claims to be the 'best attraction in Shropshire'. It is a park and woodland area, with caves, cliffs and a castle – providing a great day out (telephone: 01939 200300).

Continuing along your path, near the edge of the woods, you will reach a cross path (the route of the Shropshire Way) but keep straight on.

❺   Reach a narrow road and Grinshill Quarry, the only remaining quarry working for the sandstone. The quarries in the hill have provided rock for a vast number of buildings including Buildwas Abbey, Viroconium, Chequers, central Shrewsbury and several places in the USA. Turn right to reach a car park (Corbet Wood Picnic Area). Cross to the left side of this car park and into a sunken track, where you turn right and begin to go quite steeply downhill. Where this sunken track levels off slightly at the junction of paths, take a very sharp left dog leg and continue the descent, still in a sunken track. The steep slope is clothed by many fine trees including Scots pine, though there are more of the deciduous variety so the walk will be much more open in winter. At the bottom of the slope, the path swings round to the right. Follow a horizontal track, with gardens and then open fields to the left and a steep wooded slope on the right. Reach a short stretch of paved way, and then join a path coming from the right – the Shropshire Way seen at the top of the hill. Turn left and soon reach the village hall, and your starting point.